# BEST INTERESTS
## —— *of the* ——
# CHILDREN

*American's Dependency System as seen
through the Eyes of Guardians*

ROBERT AND MIRIAM FERTIG

Copyright © 2024 Fertig's Christian Trust, LLC.
Edited by Miriam A. Fertig, M.A.

All rights reserved. No part of this book may be reproduced, stored, or transmitted by any means—whether auditory, graphic, mechanical, or electronic—without written permission of both publisher and author, except in the case of brief excerpts used in critical articles and reviews. Unauthorized reproduction of any part of this work is illegal and is punishable by law.

**Best Interest of the Child:** A standard the court uses in deciding the disposition of a case following an adjudication of abuse or neglect, or following Termination of Parental Rights (TPR) proceedings. It is the standard that the *Guardian ad Litem* (GAL) or *Court Appointed Special Advocate* (CASA) volunteers use in choosing a course of advocacy for every child. *Guardian ad Litem* is Latin for *"Guardian at Law."* The person appointed by the court judge to look out legally for the best interest of the child. It involves the child's physical, emotional, social, psychological, medical and essential family needs.

**CASA:** Court Appointed Special Advocates for Children. CASA is a network of nearly 1,000 community-based programs that recruit, train and support citizen-volunteers to advocate for the Best Interest of abused and neglected children in courtrooms and communities. They are volunteer advocates—empowered directly by the courts—and offer judges critical information they need to ensure that each child's rights and needs are met while in foster care. Many volunteers try to stay with children until placed in loving permanent homes. For many neglected and abused children, a CASA or Guardian ad Litem volunteer is the only constant adult presence in their lives.

This book is from the author's personal experiences and notes. These were real cases. The events described in this work are true. To assure anonymity, individuals discussed are composites and all names and identifying characteristics of people, time and places were changed. *Guardian ad Litem* and C.A.S.A. did not sponsor this book.

ISBN: 979-8-89419-467-7 (sc)
ISBN: 979-8-89419-468-4 (hc)
ISBN: 979-8-89419-469-1 (e)

Because of the dynamic nature of the Internet, any web addresses or links contained in this book may have changed since publication and may no longer be valid. The views expressed in this work are solely those of the author and do not necessarily reflect the views of the publisher, and the publisher hereby disclaims any responsibility for them.

One Galleria Blvd., Suite 1900, Metairie, LA 70001
(504) 702-6708

# CONTENTS

Preface ..................................................................................1
Introduction ...........................................................................5
Guardian ad Litem Mission.................................................13
Multi-Cultural-ism...............................................................27
Case Histories ......................................................................34

| | | |
|---|---|---|
| 1 | The Snake Oil Case ............................................... | 37 |
| 2 | Clueless Case.......................................................... | 42 |
| 3 | Defiant Teen Case.................................................. | 46 |
| 4 | Lost in the System Case......................................... | 48 |
| 5 | Pattern of Denial Case .......................................... | 59 |
| 6 | Mentally Challenged Case...................................... | 64 |
| 7 | Tough Love Case.................................................... | 69 |
| 8 | Baby Machine Case................................................ | 73 |
| 9 | Troubled Lake Case................................................ | 77 |
| 10 | Sociopath Case....................................................... | 81 |
| 11 | Disadvantaged Case ............................................... | 89 |
| 12 | Hard & Soft Judges................................................ | 110 |
| 13 | Foster Care............................................................. | 114 |
| 14 | Drugs, Sex & Violence .......................................... | 123 |
| 15 | Sexual Abuse of Children ...................................... | 126 |
| 16 | Societal Solutions .................................................. | 132 |
| 17 | Adoption Process................................................... | 143 |
| 18 | Home Studies......................................................... | 150 |
| 19 | Juvenile & Adult Justice ........................................ | 158 |
| 20 | Convicts & Converts.............................................. | 166 |

| 21 | Guardian Effectiveness | 170 |
| 22 | Challenges & Solutions | 173 |
| 23 | Pre-Emptive Action | 181 |
| 24 | Motivations & Incentives | 185 |

Epilogue ........................................................................ 207
Appendix ...................................................................... 216
Generic JR Report ....................................................... 221
Termination of Parental Rights (Generic) ................ 226
Illinois DCFS Children's Cases .................................. 238
About the Authors ...................................................... 257

# PREFACE

## The Case that Changed America

Source: Brenda Barnes (Edited for this book)

In 1864, a child was born in the poorest area of New York City, named Mary Ellen. She was loved and nurtured during the early months of her life. Then her father, Thomas Wilson, was killed in the Civil War and her mother could not work and care for her. She boarded Mary Ellen with a woman who took in infants. This was common at the time.

Several months passed and Mrs. Wilson could no longer pay Mary Ellen's caretaker and she stopped coming to visit. The woman took the toddler to the Department of Charities and abandoned her there. Children were housed in abominable conditions and many did not survive. Mary and Thomas McCormack became the child's legal guardians when he came and claimed to be Mary Ellen's biological father. She was released into their custody at the age of eighteen months and was *legally* to be their "indentured servant" until the age of eighteen.

Thomas McCormack died several months later and Mary McCormack soon remarried Francis Connelly. She systematically abused the little girl. Beaten with a horsewhip, and burned, while also exposed to extreme weather, when Mr. Connelly went to work, the neighbors testified to the abuse but no one officially interfered.

Kept indoors and never allowed outside, Mary Ellen did not own shoes and had only one dress, which she wore constantly. Beaten if she even looked out the window, Mary Ellen was locked in a small closet when

Mrs. Connelly left the apartment. This child was severally abused and mistreated for seven years.

Then the family moved to another building. A neighbor heard the child's cries and became alarmed, fearing for her very life. This woman was ill and bedridden. Only a thin wall was between her room and the Connelly's apartment, so she clearly heard the abuse happening and the child begged for mercy.

When a mission worker, named Etta Wheeler, came to visit the sick woman, she related her concerns for the little girl and asked the missionary to help her. After several attempts, Mrs. Wheeler gained brief access to the apartment and saw a gaunt, bruised, burned Mary Ellen. She had on a thin, worn dress, no stockings or shoes, though it was a cold New York winter. She was horrified and determined to help the little girl. For the next months, Mrs. Wheeler sought help from police and other authorities to no avail. **(Children were treated as property, like slaves and cattle at that time, and courts would not generally intervene in any matter that was considered private).**

Finally, Mrs. Wheeler's niece suggested she contact the *American Society for Prevention of Cruelty to Animals*, stating, "She is a little animal surely." Mrs. Wheeler was desperate and went to Mr. Bergh, founder of the Society. He listened to her story but said he could do nothing without proof of abuse. The devoted Mrs. Wheeler went back to NYC's "Hell's Kitchen" tenement and received written statements from residents, including the sick woman, Mary Smitt.

When Mr. Bergh, founder of the society, read the evidence, he sent an employee to verify it with his own eyes. The man pretended to be a census taker and allowed into the apartment where he saw battered Mary Ellen. He reported back to Henry Bergh, who took immediate action and filed a petition to remove the child from the home.

While he used NY SPCA attorneys, Mr. Bergh made it clear, he was pursuing this case as a concerned citizen and it was *not* an animal abuse matter. Mr. Bergh was a highly respected member of NY society so his case was given greater attention. Court orders were prepared; within 48 hours, Mary Ellen was taken from an angry Mrs. Connelly.

The case attracted the attention of reporters and they converged upon the courthouse as Mary Ellen was carried into the judge's chambers wrapped in a blanket, as she had no coat to wear. She was still wearing the same old dress that Mrs. Wheeler had seen her in three months before. She was small, thought to be about six, but was actually ten years old.

Mary Ellen's face was disfigured and covered with welts and bruises. Mrs. Connelly had slashed the girl with scissors only the day prior. Mary Ellen was in hysterics because she did not know where she was being taken, and she had not ever been outside except for the move from one apartment to another.

Finally, she was calmed with a lollipop that a police officer bought for her and told the judge her name, which had been unknown until this time. She said she did not know her age and that she was whipped and beaten every day. She had never been kissed or comforted and was terrified of "Mama".

The court found Mrs. Connelly guilty of felonious assault and she was sent to prison for one year of hard labor. Mary Ellen eventually went to Etta Wheeler's mother where she remained until the elderly woman's death. She then went to Mrs. Wheeler's sister who cared for her until adulthood.

Mary Ellen learned to walk, became aware of moral behavior and taught about God. She had never played with any other child or owned a toy and had to learn those social skills. As the years passed, Mary Ellen became a happy girl, and a well- adjusted adult. She was married at age twenty-four to a widower and had two children. She named the eldest daughter Etta after her benefactor.

She spoke once at a conference of the *American Humane Society* in 1913. Her speech was published by the Society, entitled "*The Story of Mary Ellen*," which started a *Child Saving Crusade throughout America*. Because of Mary Ellen, Henry Bergh founded the *York Society for the Prevention of Cruelty to Children*, which has saved countless lives.

Mary Ellen Wilson died in 1956 at the age of 92 surrounded by a loving family. Her rescue opened the eyes of the American public to the great issue of child abuse. Her life inspired others to make a difference and speak up for justice. Though more than a century has passed, she remains an important part of the fight to end child suffering.

**Congress created the Child Advocate System, known as *Guardian ad Litem* in 1974.**

# INTRODUCTION

Every year, there are three million reports of children neglected and abused in the United States. For every incident of child abuse or neglect reported, an estimated two incidents go unreported. Almost five children die *every day* from child abuse. More than three out of four are under the age of four. Child abuse occurs across all socioeconomic levels, all cultural lines, all religions and education level. Neglect, the most widespread form of child abuse, makes up more than 59% of all abuse cases.

Source: *Child help* and *DOSOMETHING.org*
- **Florida Population is NOW 20m; 20% or 4.2m are Children**
- **Age 60 plus is 5m or 25%; projected to double by 2030.**
- **Youth in Florida Foster Care is about 415,129**
- **About 238,230 Children Aged-Out of Foster Care**
- **Nearly 18,000 Aged-Out Without a Permanent Family**
- **There are 30,000 Cases of Child Abuse/Neglect, every year.**

Source: *www. GuardianTrusts.org*
*The public must know how our national child protection and elderly system works—or does not work—so that people can participate politically in its reform.*

Most maltreatment deaths result from physical abuse, especially children receiving injuries to their heads. Known as *abusive head trauma*, these injuries occur when a child's head is slammed against a surface, is severely struck or when a child is violently shaken. There have been major improvements in the ability to diagnose abusive head trauma and in investigators' abilities to recognize when a caregiver's explanation for injuries do not match the severity of the injuries.

These GALs had a case involving abusive head trauma to a two-year old beautiful boy. The parent dropped the baby on its head. We knew immediately, *intuitively* that the parent attempted to cover-up *an accident*. She did not fit the profile: she admitted lying to CPI; was repentant, and willing to do whatever was required to pay for her foolish lie. Nonetheless, that lie required her to complete a case plan and pay over $10,000 in services and legal costs (disadvantaged families do not pay anything). The parent attended church almost daily, to ask the Lord to forgive her for attempting to cover-up this accident. This case successfully closed. They later had other wonderful children.

Many children who die from physical abuse, have been abused over time, but a one-time event often causes a death. The most common reason given by caretakers who fatally injure their children is that they lost patience when the child would not stop crying. Other common reasons given by the abusers include bedwetting, fussy eating and disobedient behavior.

Fatalities from neglect include a number of different ways in which caregivers fail to adequately provide for or supervise their children. Caregivers may fail to provide food and nurturing to their child, leading to malnutrition, failure to thrive, starvation or dehydration. Caregivers may fail to seek medical care when their child is ill, leading to more serious illness and death. Neglect cases can also result from intentional or grossly negligent failure to adequately supervise a child, resulting in bathtub drowning, suffocations, poisonings and other types of fatal incidents.

Young children are the most vulnerable victims. National statistics show that children under six years of age account for 86% of all maltreatment deaths and infants account for 43% of these deaths. Fathers and mothers' boyfriends are most often the perpetrators of abuse; mothers are more often at fault in the neglect fatalities. Fatal abuse is interrelated with poverty, domestic violence and [usually] substance abuse.

## *Major Risk Factors*
- Younger children, especially under the age of five.
- Parents or caregivers who are under the age of 30.
- Low income, single-parent families experiencing depression and stresses.
- Children left with male caregivers who lack emotional attachment to the child.
- Children with physical, emotional and mental health problems.
- Lack of suitable childcare services.
- Substance abuse among the primary caregivers.
- Caregivers with unrealistic expectations of child development and behavior.

## *Prevention*
- Training hospital emergency room staff to improve their ability to identify child abuse fatalities and improve reporting to the appropriate agencies.
- Providing an advisory on the mandated reporting of child abuse and neglect to local human service agencies, hospitals and physicians.
- Case management, referral and follow-up of infants sent home with serious health or developmental problems.
- Media campaigns to enlighten and inform the public on known fatality-producing behaviors, i.e., violently shaking a child out of frustration.
- Crisis Nurseries which serve as havens for parents "on the edge" where they can leave their children for a specified time, at no charge.
- Intensive home visiting services to parents of at-risk infants and toddlers.

- Education programs for parents such as the Parent Effectiveness Training (P.E.T.), the Parent Nurturing Program and Systematic Training for Effective Parenting (S.T.E.P.).

    Source: National MCH Center for Child Death Review (edited for this book)

This is a *true story* from children less than ten years old. They are the most vulnerable and innocent of all children. **We were the voices for these children.** They cannot speak for themselves. This story will give the reader a portrait of how State Departments of Children and Families (DCF) system works to protect children, with the essential support of volunteers like us, known as *Guardian ad Litem (GALs) or CASA.*

GAL and CASA volunteers work without enough resources, without adequate training, with insufficient supervision, and lack of suitable state funding. These volunteers do works of charity without faith-based support because of our secularized governmental system. By this we do not mean they are atheistic; many are spiritual, but they are not permitted to express their Judeo-Christian beliefs—*Love of God and love of neighbor.*

The malevolence that we expected to experience was parent's abandonment, abuse and neglect of God's precious innocent children. While we find reasons to fault Florida's Department of Children and Families (DCF), what we *did not* expect to encounter was a far *more dysfunctional* (DCF) system in many other states—**nationwide.**

**Objectives of this work:**

(1) To inform readers about the **charitable works** of thousands of volunteers, known as GALs, who sacrifice so much for the 550,000 actually abandoned, neglected and abused children throughout America. In just two counties of Florida alone, there are 3,000-child abuse or neglect cases, and only about 700 GALs

and 100 young Case Managers (CMs) in these counties to help so many children and their troubled families.

(2) Enlighten readers about many great success stories *and* some of the shortcomings of this child dependency and justice system. This ***imperfect*** nationwide system exists to protect innocent children, and to try to help rehabilitate many misguided parents.

(3) Suggest some of the ***root causes*** of this societal predicament and propose possible innovative solutions to enhance and improve this *dysfunctional system*.

Those students who are planning a career as social workers will find Case Management (CM) most enlightening. Couples who are planning to adopt children will be better informed. Foster care families might be interested in some of the challenges they will certainly face. Finally, if you are searching for a more meaningful work of ***real charity***, you may find that goal wholly fulfilled as a *Guardian ad Litem* volunteer.

This book is *not* a replacement for excellent training documents created by others. We do not want to "rehash" what more expert writers have produced. This is a ***personal story*** that we hope will provide greater insight and motivation for future volunteers.

GAL's role is *not* to take children away from parents (as some misinformed persons presume); it is actually the reverse—it is to help parents reunite with their children. It is the Child Protection Investigator's (CPI) role to remove children from parents when warranted by *sufficient evidence* of abandonment, neglect, or abuse—*not the Guardians*.

A case begins with CPI removal of a child or children, followed by adjudication by a judge. The Department of Children and Family (DCF) Services then creates a case plan for the parents. Children may then live with a relative caregiver or foster care family. At this stage of the process, a Guardian ad Litem might be assigned to the case—if and only if, critical resources and volunteers are available to support the case.

This book examines the key parental, family, cultural and spiritual challenges in our society that have influenced and will continue to shape how we look at the "family nucleus." More than 75% of Americans claim to be Judeo-Christians, at the beginning of the 21$^{st}$ century (down from 85%, a short decade ago). Our American Constitution and Bill of Rights is based on Christian values as its fundamental foundation.

*We are "persons." We must build human relationships. We do not win for the children by debates or arguments alone—but by our examples of charity. Love them! Pray for them!*

All children are born good, innocent and lovable! It is the parents, the relatives and role models, as well as peer groups, teachers, and especially the *"culture of death"* that causes *some* of these children to grow-up to be dysfunctional, and in many cases become "bad parents" themselves.

What do we mean by "culture of death?" It consists of many factors: the 55% divorce rate; explicit violence and sex in movies, electronic games and on the internet; "paramours" (so-called lovers that live together) who do not take responsibility for their children. In addition, abortion-on-demand has caused millions of late-term deaths annually (an estimated 54 million cumulative abortions, since Roe vs. Wade). In addition, the abuse of alcohol, drugs and pills has become a national epidemic.

> *We have met the enemy—and he is us.*
> —Walt Kelly

The lack of spiritual formation (Jewish, Christian, among other faiths) was absent in about 85% of our cases, and that represents one of the most important reasons for the serious breakdown of social order within American (and Western) society. Conversely, we must be very careful to avoid *extreme fundamentalists* that will actually create further issues for children. *Individual and group evil really exists!* If you question this, read *People of the Lie*, by Dr. Scott Peck, which proves this fact beyond any reasonable doubt.

Many parents are clueless. They have no idea about the fundamentals of parenting. They are immature adults themselves. As one Judge said, "they are like rabbits that keep on reproducing." Immature adults should *not* have children, if they are not prepared physically, psychologically, morally, to be loving parents. Can you really love as a parent, if you have not been loved as a child? The answer is yes—if, and only if, you get proper therapy and loving care as a child before one becomes an adult.

*The first and best victory is to conquer self.*
—Plato

Guardian *"ad Litem"* (GAL) means **"Guardian at law, for the court case."** It is an old concept in—in Anglo-Saxon times, at common law, the King of England appointed a person to speak on behalf of a child or incompetent adults. They are volunteers that willingly give of their time, talent, and treasure *without* any compensation. Why do GALs do it? What is their motivation? We can only speak for ourselves. For us it is simple: we do it to prevent child tragedies, such as those more sensationalized reports found in this book. We try to *save one child at a time*. We do this work to serve our Lord's precious little ones.' We try, with His grace, to follow the two most important commandments: *Love of God, and love of neighbor.*

**Basic Needs of Children:** (*Maslow's Hierarchy of Needs*, by Alan Chapman)

1. **Biological Welfare**: Food, shelter, health, clothes, clean air, sleep and water;

2. **Safety & Security:** Protection, domestic order, stability, sense of security;

3. **Love & Belonging:** Parental bonding, family relationships, positive role models;

4. **Self Esteem:** Personal responsibility, achievement, status, reputation;

5. **Cognitive:** Knowledge, finding meaning, self-awareness;

6. **Aesthetic:** Beauty, balance, form, sounds and colors;

7. **Self-actualization:** Personal growth, sexual development, fulfillment;

8. **Transcendence:** By helping, others self-actualize.

What does Chapman mean by *self-actualize*? Does he mean, "Someone's perceived personality," or one's own individual interests and welfare, especially when placed before those of other people?" as the Dictionary defines it? If this is his meaning, then it suggests one's self-esteem or ego is more important, not self-sacrificing for others.

# GUARDIAN AD LITEM MISSION

*Democracy put man on a pedestal; feminism put women on a pedestal. But neither democracy nor feminism could live a generation out unless a child was put on a pedestal.*
—Fulton J. Sheen

There are about 30,000 (on average) children in the Child Welfare Dependency system in Florida alone, during the last five years, with only 8,000 *Guardian ad Litem* volunteers statewide. Our mission is protecting children by advocating for them in the courts. We also try to help children's parents with **Reunification**: to make sure that essential child needs are available when parents re-unite with their children, *after* they have completed a case plan.

If reunification is not possible, after 9-12 months of parents working their case plan tasks, the alternative goal is to find a **Permanent Caregiver**, hopefully a relative, to care for the children.

If these goals are not achievable, the Guardian (GAL), Case Manager (CM) and the State (ADA), recommend to the Judge, **Termination of Parental Rights (TPR)**, which eventually results in adoption of the child or children.

Our goal is the **Best Interest of the Children**—it is not just about the parents.

The author and co-author, my spouse of more than fifty years, worked as GAL volunteers for five years. During this time, we handled thirteen cases involving twenty-five children. This volunteer work required many discussions with caregivers and visitations to foster care providers. We interviewed schoolteachers, had serious deliberations with caseworkers and their supervisors. We spoke to police officers, doctors, and reviewed therapists reports. We interviewed psychologists, had consultations with GAL attorneys, and had numerous appearances before judges.

We were required to visit *all* the children once a month, and produce visitation reports. GALs are required to write detailed Judicial Reviews (JRs) every five months. Supervisors and lawyers review these JRs, before distributing them to the judge, Assistant DA, parent's lawyers, and Case Managers, before the court hearing.

We are retired seniors, so we were able to work 2-3 cases at one time. Full-time working persons might take on 1-2 cases at a time; much depends on the complexity of the case. We *avoided* child sexual abuse cases because it would be extremely difficult for us to maintain our objectivity. We also shunned teenage cases because once those teenage hormones kick-in, it can be (is) very difficult (we have dealt with three of our own teenagers, so we knew something about teen challenges). Other more competent, patient GALs handle those demanding cases.

We select our cases from a synopsis of histories, based on what we think we can handle. One has to assess his or her own particular strengths *and weaknesses*. We admire GALs who are capable of handling far more difficult, special needs cases, like physically or mentally challenged children.

We have rarely felt threatened as Guardians—except by one parent and a few defense lawyers. The State protects volunteers from lawsuits related to cases, except of course where one intentionally commits a serious crime. All GALs must have a clean record (we are thoroughly checked-out for any past criminal activities), and we need to have a charitable attitude—*an attitude of gratitude*. It should be obvious that one really cares for children. If one does not naturally love children, they are in the wrong vocation. Most GALs were parents or grandparents themselves (exceptions always exist).

We receive about 30 hours of excellent training. However, this is only the *"end-of-the-beginning."* One needs to study the training materials after the formal classes are completed, and we are now required to attend twelve focused, 2-3 hour update sessions yearly. All GALs are *re-certified* each year. We all must agree to protect confidential information. Perhaps the most difficult part of being a Guardian is letting go of *"your children,"* especially if it takes years before your particular case is finally closed.

Below is a "generalized" chart that shows inter-relationships between organizations:

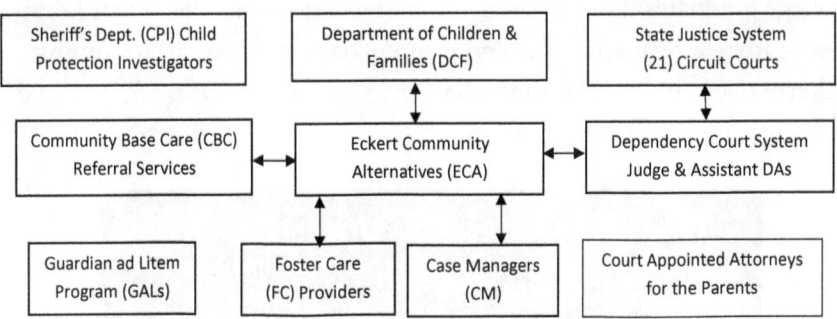

CPI, GALs, ECA and ADA are independent organizations. Independence (ideally) provides some degree of checks and balances between the various groups. Court appointed attorneys for the parents are also independent. All interface with the Head of DCF, who reports to the Governor. Legislature oversees and approves DCF budgets.

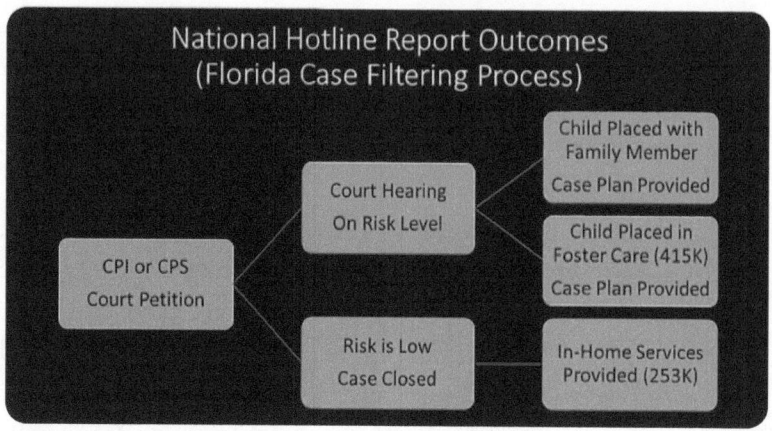

Caseworkers or managers (CMs), who interface with GALs, are generally fresh out of college. About 80-85% of them are young women. The CM is directly responsible for their assigned cases. The typical caseworker is perhaps 25-35 years old, has a college degree, and is perhaps too young to have much parenting experience. These young, enthusiastic college graduates typically have too many cases to handle. Their heavy caseloads cause many to become disenchanted. Eckerd Community Alternatives (ECA), the umbrella organization, has *allegedly* reduced this ridiculous caseload problem.

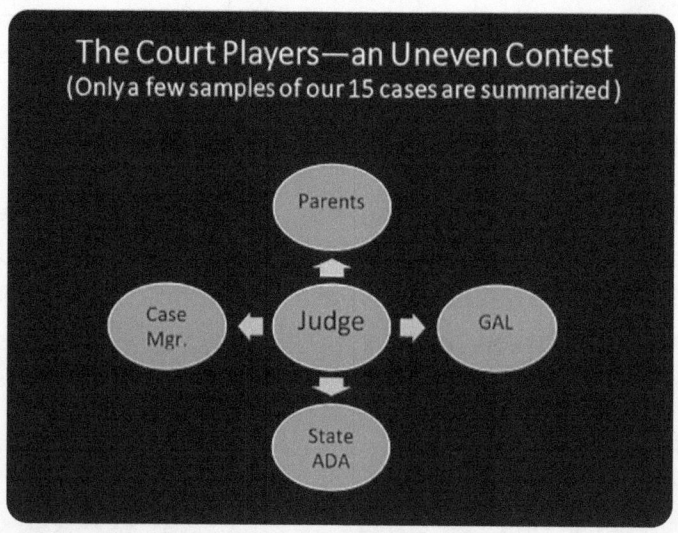

In recent years, Case Management (CM) turnover rate has been enormous, as high as 70-80% per year, causing serious problems, straining an already *dysfunctional* system. No business can function with such a high turnover rate. CMs are required to visit caregivers and children twice each month. They must write detailed reports on *everything* related to the family and the children (consuming about 60% of their time). They interface with us GALs, the state Assistant DA, other specialists, professionals, and mostly with the parents and children, and they finally must report to the court.

Unfortunately, many of the more capable CMs move on to other more rewarding job opportunities elsewhere, and less gifted CMs get burnt-out and eventually leave—*or worse*--they get promoted to higher management positions, where they can do (have done) some very serious damage to an already national *dysfunctional* system.

Supervisors or coordinators of GALs are typically responsible for 40-50 volunteers. These skilled, underpaid managers might be responsible for up to 80 cases, involving over 130 children. They typically must respond to numerous urgent crises, and do not have much time available to consider future "preventive action."

GAL lawyers handle up to 150 cases (200-300 children). They review all official reports and suggest changes, although Guardians have the final responsibility for report content that does not directly concern the law. Our experience with these dedicated, over-worked, and under-paid lawyers (except in one case), has been *extremely positive.*

GALs have one agenda: ***The Manifest Best Interest of the Children.***

We are on the "front-line" in the life of these children. We speak for them in the court. We keep them safe with parents, or foster care providers, and within their environment. We empower the family, through the CM, by recommending referrals that can help them. We suggest reasonable choices for the parents, while being sensitive to different family backgrounds, diverse cultures and historical traditions. We may propose options for those directly involved in the case. GALs must find out what the child and parent concerns are by carefully listening to them and observing their "body language," while giving them opportunities to listen to and understand us.

We review confidential medical and police reports about the parents, interface with caregivers, and the children, *only* after getting signed releases from the parents or their primary caregivers. We check on referrals; e.g., substance abuse, domestic violence or anger management classes, parenting courses, therapy treatments, day care services, relative caregiver funds, etc. We do not take anything on its face value. We are reporters of the facts: this is what we have observed, or heard or read from a specifically named source. We must obtain as much of this information as possible *firsthand* in order to give the judge objective facts, *not opinions*. Individual life experiences form an important part of our daily decisions, which we must always (somehow) try to keep in check.

Summaries of these reports and direct conversations with experts become vital inputs to our monthly Visitation Reports, Judicial Reviews (JRs), every five months, and Termination of Parental Report (TPR), among other official court documents. We make *recommendations* based upon our independent inquiries. We do not normally do police-like investigations. We synthesize information from various sources: police, doctors, therapists, teachers, daycare providers, parents, relatives, foster parents, and review all earlier historical files related to our particular case.

GALs are reporters of facts. We are the **"*objective eyes and ears of the judge.*"** We do not form conclusions; that is the Judge's role. Unlike others, who may be motivated, measured, and paid based on different sets of criteria our *only* focus is: **"*The Best Interest of the Children.*"**

| Comparison: | Guardian ad Litem | vs. | Eldercare Guardians |
|---|---|---|---|
| • Training: | 30-plus 12 hrs. per yr. | | 40-plus 8 hrs. per yr. |
| • Court Time: | JR (5$^{th}$ Mo.), TPR | | As Needed |
| • Visitations: | Once/mo. | | Once/mo. |
| • Reporting: | Monthly | | Yearly |
| • Authority: | Limited | | Court Defined |
| • Services: | Volunteer | | Paid by Clients |

What if parents do not know much about morality, decency, or right from wrong behavior, who is then responsible? Public schools do not primarily focus on or teach morality. One has to teach good behavior to children *very early in life*. Without good behavior, where are they? Where are we? Someone must step in and teach the children basic fundamental morality. Today's new Paganism is self-exaltation of man and woman. It comes in various forms, such as secularism, rationalism, relativism, progressivism and materialism.

Consider the views from retired Judge Sullivan, these GALs court judge, and author of *Raised by the Courts*: "In 2006, in Nassau County, NY, nearly two million teens, under age 18 were arrested, most were abusing drugs and alcohol. ... An estimated 80% of all teens in the Juvenile Justice system are under the influence of drugs, while committing crimes. Nearly 85% of youths treated for substance abuse also have mental disorders. Every dollar spent on addiction treatment, saves about $4-7 on drug-related crimes. Female youths are the fastest growing population in the Juvenile Justice system; they represent about 1/3$^{rd}$ of arrests and 1/4$^{th}$ of today's incarcerations."

## Parental Case Plans

Case plans created by Eckerd Community Alternatives (ECA), the umbrella organization in charge of case managers, and various state contract referral services, are commonly developed *without* much input from GALs because we typically get involved later in the case process.

ECA provides detailed checklists of tasks to be complete by parents in order for them to demonstrate to the court that they are ready for reunification with their children. If they cannot "get their act together," after about 9-12 months, the legal process goes to the next step.

## Juvenile Court Processes

The juvenile legal process involves about 12-17 steps, summarized below:

1. **Initial report.** Claim of abuse/neglect is reported to the CPI from **Hotline or 911**. CPI investigates ONLY if the caller reporting *"appears to be creditable."*

2. **Petition filed by CPI.** The children may be taken into temporary custody, within 12-24 hours, depending on the situation and judge's order.

3. **Non-secure custody hearing.** Happens 1-7 days after removal of the children.

4. **On-going non-secure custody hearing.** Occurs within 7 days, and every 30 days thereafter, as the investigation continues. Children's placement and services are determined. A GAL could be assigned depending on available of resources.

5. **Prehearing conference.** Discussion by CPI, the DA, parent's attorneys, and GAL attorney, take place to try to settle the allegations; e.g., the accused may plead guilty and attempt to make a case plan deal with the DA at this stage.

6. **Adjudication hearing**. Held within 60 days from filing the original petition. All parties present evidence and examine witness. A Judge determines if allegations by CPI have been proven. GAL *management* assures the court that it has reviewed or confirmed the

facts and recommends professional services needed by the children, the family, and the CM discusses what services should be provided.

7. **Dispositional hearing.** CPI and CM develop a Case Plan for the family. The plan is given within three months to the caregivers, *with/without GAL* involvement depending on volunteer resources. *This is a key potential problem.* In the last 3 ½ years, this GAL attended only one disposition hearing. I was also discouraged from asking questions at this meeting. GALs should be involved in *case plan creation much earlier*; otherwise, we might have to petition the judge later with motions requesting a court order to modify the case plan, after providing evidence and factual reasons why the case plan needs to be changed.

8. **Ongoing out-of-court involvement.** At this stage, GAL typically selects the case, and assigned by the judge. We prefer to see a synopsis of the case upfront, before selecting it, to be certain we have the ability to handle the case.

9. **First Judicial Review hearing.** Within 90 days of the dispositional hearing, the CM and GAL are required to present their first JR.

10. **Second and subsequent JR hearings.** About 5-6 months later another JR is required to keep the judge informed on case progress (or lack thereof). GAL and the CM may/may not agree on the progress of the caregivers and children's status. It is important to try to resolve our differences *outside* of court, and not *"throw anyone under the bus."* Although it happens, when the CM/GAL do not do their work fully or have not provided essential services for the parties.

11. **Permanency hearing.** This court hearing is required within 9-12 months after removal of the children, and after subsequent hearings at least every 5-6 months. GAL and CM then advocate for a safe, permanent family home for the children, by recommending Permanent Guardianship, or Adoption, after TPR.

12. **Termination of Parental Rights (TPR).** The parents or caregivers have 30 days to file a reply to a TPR request by the CM/GAL. The judge then orders mitigation.

13. **Mitigation.** A meeting between the DA, CM, GAL, the parents, and lawyers for all sides, takes place under a court appointed "neutral" expert, who attempts to mitigate the issues to avoid TPR, if possible. If all sides come to an agreement, they all sign the document, before sending it to the judge for his/her "official" approval. We have had an agreement that the judge did not accept.

14. **TPR trial.** All parties prepare for the TPR trial before the judge, typically within 30-60 days. Attorneys for all sides (DA, CM, GAL, parents, and expert witnesses, gather evidence and prepare their clients for trial. The authors have been involved in two TPR trials. *Preparation is crucial!* Typically, a few days or weeks before trial, a huge pile of discovery documents arrives for your examination. We had to sift through two feet of papers to find 2-3 key documents for facts that were relevant to the case. At this critical stage, we believe in turning off all phones and finding a quiet conference room to go over ALL the evidence with our GAL lawyer, plan the strategy, and finalize our TPR report, in order to win the case for the Best Interest of the Children. *Rehearsals are absolutely essential!*

Note: Although TPR cases are very challenging to prepare for and win, they are usually "black or white" cases; they are not in the "gray scale" of events. If it gets to the TPR stage the parent(s) are not doing their case plan, they are not cooperating, and they have probably failed to care for their children. The GAL, the assistant DA, the CM and the legal team have to prove the case by *"clear and convincing evidence."* The *alleged* culpable parents are *not* required to prove their case. Defense trial lawyers do not have to provide witnesses or put the parents on the witness stand. The typically court-appointed attorneys are often excellent.

15. **Post TPR Appeal.** Parents have a legal right to Appeal the judge's decision within 30 days. They need a special Appeals lawyer who usually argues issues about the law. They typically do not contest the facts of the case, only "interpretation of the law." Appeals can take many months by the higher court. Meanwhile the potential adopting parents have to have enormous patience, and pray that appeal will be denied. Waiting a year is not unrealistic.

16. **Post-TPR Review**. Judge hears from CM and GAL about permanency plans.

17. **Adoption Petition.** Children are placed for adoption within six months of termination. GAL requests information on the adoption selection from CM. GAL may elect to monitor the case, or move on to another case.

## Case Plan Staffing

Parent(s) have staffing meetings with all concerned parties, where ECA (Eckerd Community Alternatives) formally presents all of the tasks to be completed and their goals. GALs attend these meetings, especially if we are actively involved. After the meeting the parent(s) sign-off on their plan, where they essentially agree *legally* to all that it contains and its goals. It is lately getting better, but in the past, Staffing meetings were absurd: they rarely started on time (lack of respect for other people's time); the supervisor types a report with her back to GAL; and reports contained many misspellings and too often serious factual errors.

These case plans are reasonable for the majority of the parent(s), but *some are not*. We attended one case plan presentation, which was *not* reasonable. We were told not to voice objections in front of the parents. It was an unreasonable presentation because the mother did not know what in hell they were talking about: she was certified *"mentally disadvantaged,"* and ECA knew that clear fact in advance of their presentation.

In addition, the child's aunt, the primary caregiver at that time, sat in on this meeting and told us afterward that, *"this meeting was crazy!"* GAL agreed with her assessment. We told the aunt that they have to do this for "legal reasons," in order to demonstrate to the judge that the parents freely and legally accepted their particular case plan. Moreover, the mother's mental condition might be treatable by doctors and drugs.

Parents may do some or most of their case plan tasks. The CM, GAL, ADA and the Court, during JR hearings, determine if they are "non-compliant," "partly-compliant," or "fully-compliant." Obviously, this is partly objective and subjective call by the judge. In many cases, the judge decided to allow the case to close, because of the state's high caseload and rising costs, or close a "partly-compliant" case, if it *appears* that the parents are making progress. If the judge is wrong, the case ends up back in the system. If parents are reunited prematurely, it usually causes added trauma for their children.

This actually happened in one of our cases, which could have been catastrophic. One parent did 75%, and another only did about 25% of their case plan tasks, but the ADA, the CM and the Judge allowed them to reunite with the children, even though GAL *strongly objected*. We asked, "Why have case plans, if the parents can get off so easily with only *partly* completed tasks; just because they appear to be making progress?" Our observation, experiences and *gut feelings* told us that these young parents were not ready for reunification (gut feelings or intuition does *not* count in any court justice system, but one should never, never ignore your instincts).

A week before the parents reunited with their children, both tested positive for cocaine. Subsequently, because of other illegal activities their rights to the children were later terminated (TPR), after a full trial, where GAL, together with CM, the Assistant DA, and GAL attorney (parents were represented by court–appointed lawyers), showed by *overwhelming evidence,* lack of parental responsibility. This difficult case finally ended. Both children were adopted a year later by loving and responsible parents. We felt sad for the biological parents; it is not easy to be involved in the separation of *any* young mom and dad from their children. Yet it is not GAL, but the judge who makes that essential final decision. We prayed for those misguided parents.

Faith-based therapy might be an important *alternative* to for future case plans. Obviously, this is an "outside-the-box" idea, which *needs to be voluntary*, and financed with private funds. Field test cases could determine if *optional* faith-based case planning tasks really reduces repeat offenders, and saves significant taxpayer money. If faith-based therapy really works, shouldn't the state be willing to find a way around the *so-called* "separation of state and religion" clause?

The Constitution actually says, "Congress shall make no law respecting an establishment of religion, or prohibiting the free exercise thereof." John Adams further stated, *"Our Constitution was made only for moral and religious people. It is wholly inadequate to the government of any other."*

Many CM's we worked with are gifted, dedicated and capable professionals, but *a few were not*. Most CM's are college graduates with a mix of academic courses: psychology, mental health, special education, counseling case studies, child development, and communication skills, among other important skills. Many use their CM experiences at ECA to go on to achieve their ultimate career path goals, whatever they may be. The State cannot continue to expect young college adults with little or no experience in *real-life* parent-child situations, to handle 30-35 cases per month. That is *unrealistic,* and creates a "revolving door" dysfunctional situation in the DCF dependency system.

The turnover at ECA is extremely high. We have had some cases where the CM changed 3-5 times within one month, with the same case. This situation exists because (among other reasons) these young case managers cannot possibly handle such unrealistic caseloads. They ultimately "burn-out!" It is as if someone throws you into a pool and says, "Try swimming!" They are afraid to sink, so he or she paddles along rapidly, and somehow survives, *for now*. The children suffer most under such ludicrous conditions. Two months (on average) are added to the case timeframe each time a new CM is assigned to a case, since it takes that long to get up to speed on the case.

# MULTI-CULTURAL-ISM

What is culture? It is a much-abused word in today's Western and American society. Culture that is *civilized* does not sanction immoral behavior (substance abuse, violence, and irresponsible sex), nor does it support repulsive language or loud fanatical music (as in *some* Hip-Hop music), nor does it allow gross dress code (pants that do not cover ones' butt), or forms of repugnant modern art, and revolting anti-social manners.

Culture in society includes traditions, customs, languages, religions, history, and institutions for the sciences, arts and music. It is based on moral values that we treasure in any civilized society.

In general, culture refers to what we honor and worship in our society; it's the system of behavioral phenomena that is dependent upon social and symbolic learning, consisting of shared understanding, communicated from generation to generation, structured according to its own set of virtuous rules for society and based on laws that are just.

## Symbolism

One of the most important elements of any culture is the grammatical character of symbols, combined to make complicated utterances for the purpose of communicating and storing information. This aspect of symbolism also makes it possible for us to consider things in the abstract, without the requirement that we go through an actual physical process of trial and error. A practical example is the use of mathematics symbols, where by performing symbolic operations with numbers, one can be certain that one kind of bridge design will stand whereas another will not.

## Multi-Cultural Societies

Qualitatively, various aspects of patterned behavior form interacting systems. Changes in one portion of the system will tend to produce compensating changes elsewhere. One major source of change is the chronic need of adjusting to the environment within the society. Any given culture will, eventually feel the impact of contact with one or more other cultures, and the resultant flow of traits will occasion change. Examples include the Hispanic influence on American culture, and significant Islamic impact on the European culture.

## Dominant Cultures

Although the evolution of culture seems to have a higher potential for reversible movements, the available record of global cultural evolution indicates that there has been a more or less consistent development in the direction of higher complexity. There is a significant function for dominant types—those culture-types which tend to spread at the expense of others. The dominant culture tends to overwhelm the others, causing members to develop greater resemblance to the dominant type, but often creating hybrid developments that are new dominants.

Certain cultures, *in general*, like Jewish, Asians (Japanese in particular), and Muslims, seem to have fewer problems with substance abuse, violent crime, neglect and abuse of children (exceptions always exist). Why is it true for these cultures compared with countless Anglo-Saxons? Argumentatively it is due to greater respect for parents, stricter family morals, education, and faith or trust in God, among other factors.

## Asian Cultures

During my earlier business travels to the Orient (seven times to Japan), I found Asians extraordinary in terms of family values and individual ethics. For example, I accidentally left my coat on a department store counter, which contained all my money, credit cards and passport, at a shopping mall in Tokyo. Hours later, I found the coat with its contents intact where I left it. That would not happen in America.

Why do many Asians, in general, act more ethically (again, exceptions exist)? We believe that, from early childhood they learn morality and respect for the family. To steal or to perform immoral acts is a "disgrace," for the individual *and* the entire family. "Exceptional-ism" is another trait of proud Asians. Why do IBM, GE, Microsoft, and other huge corporations, employ Asian foreigners to handle intricate online computer problems and other complex services, from far away countries, such as India and the Philippines? Obviously, it is primarily because of lower cost, but also significant is that there are large populations of self-motivated and highly skilled work forces, that offers these corporations the essential *quality* of service that customers demand.

## African-American Culture

(Classifications of race such as "black and white," or "person of color" is imprecise. Almost 80% of the world's population of seven billion people is non-white).

The star of *Runaway Slave* is Rev. C.L. Bryant. It's a documentary, in which the star of the film, Bryant interviews African-American politicians, holds meetings with community activists, and discovers the little known "other" history of the Civil Rights Movement.

"Runaway Slave exposes the NAACP as a mouthpiece of the Democratic Party, and the NAACP's leaders as the ultimate 'race hustlers' who perpetuate—and profit—from a *'victim mentality'* [emphasis mine] that hurts the African-American community.

"The theme of Runaway Slave is compelling: while the African-American community has triumphed over the scourge of physical slavery, many still suffer from a *mental slavery*—to government [dependency]. What emerges from this posit is an authentic and honest discussion of race in America, a discussion Americans need to have together."

"There is a *50-year-old lie* that has caused an entire people to become harlots to the *political idea that government knows what is best*," declares Bryant.

Our research has shown that about 73% of African-American children have only one parent, typically the mother. *That is an appalling statistic!* We believe most of these families have collapsed because of government policies that *encouraged* one-parent families: When fathers cannot cope with being real fathers to their children, government welfare takes over. That is a creeping and deleterious form of government dependency.

## Hispanic Culture

Hispanics or Latinos have been part of the American culture centuries before the Pilgrims arrived. Spanish-speaking people represent 15% of the population. Unlike Asians and Anglo-Saxons, one might claim that Hispanics are more "impulse driven;" that is, they are particularly emotional about family, religion, and historical traditions. Their inability to speak and read English is a major factor in their lack of assimilation, especially Mexican-Americans. Many have somehow risen above this communication failing. Education is the solution to future adaptation for this proud culture. Hispanics should be more politically involved to address issues prevalent in their communities. It is interesting to see how the Cubans succeeded after coming to America with extremely limited resources and poor English skills. Perhaps they "over-compensated" for the many hardships they had endured in Cuba, and they are clearly more politically active.

## Islamic Culture

> *Those without faith, one must start with human reason. When arguing with Muslims or Pagans it does no good to quote the Bible. Contra Gentiles*
> by Thomas Aquinas

Muslims currently represent only about two percent of the American population, but they are growing rapidly. Most are blameless conservative families, who instruct their children from a very early age to be moral and obedient to the father—*or else!*

Conversely, Islamic cultures in many Muslim countries have *very harsh* treatment for offenders. If you steal, you will lose a hand or your arm. Commit adultery, or show that you are openly gay, and you will lose your head. Islam does **not** accept the American Bill of Rights. That fundamental law is foreign to their culture, faith and *Sharia* laws.

Muslims have a rapidly increasing population, many times greater than most other cultures, and have a growing majority in some cities in America (such as Detroit). Most Muslims are conservative and live peacefully together with Christians and other cultures, and they follow our civil laws. On the other hand, there are *fundamentalist* who are stuck in the ancient 7$^{th}$ century world, and they want to establish parallel societies with *Sharia* law, which is *incompatible* with many Western and American laws.

Liberal democracies in Europe and America gave sanctuary to Muslims from recent war torn countries in Afghanistan, Iraq and the Middle East. America expected immigrants to assimilate into their place of residence. *Assimilation has not occurred!* Traditional primeval Muslim customs still exists, not merely veils for woman, but also polygamy, parental arranged marriages, wife beatings, and ritual circumcision of young girls.

Demographics and economics are exacerbating this problem. Americans are not having many babies as young couples. They are more concerned with their upward mobility; that is, "keeping up with the Jones's." (American birth rates recently dropped to 1.9 births per couple). In contrast, Muslims are propagating at a phenomenal rate. These conditions make Western and American cities, subject to greater violence. In France, Muslim suburbs of Paris and other cities erupted into riots with young people battling with the police, looting and setting fires. In London, trains and buses were bombed. In an effort to deal with this problem, authorities in Western cities are de facto ceding control of particular regions to Muslim inhabitants; e.g., Berlin, Manchester, and Paris suburbs. With current demographics trends, these problems will continue to worsen.

## Liberian Culture

The Liberian community in Staten Island, NYC has been involved in a string of government lobbying campaigns since the 1990s to extend the "Deferred Enforced Departure" (DED) status, which President Clinton has had deferred on a yearly basis by presidential order for immigrants who fled the Liberian war without immigration visas. There are about 3,600 Liberians in America, who are on DED status.

This new wave of immigrates settled in Staten Island in the Park Hill Projects. As the civil war intensified, more immigrants followed, creating a community with African restaurants and businesses, and others working and building businesses in NYC, notably in Brooklyn. In recent years, Liberian families have been settling in nearby New Jersey, with a large community in the Trenton, New Jersey. Many of these families are Muslims or Christians. Most do *not* have birth certificates; some were born in the bush! Result: numerous adults get foster care as children (nobody knows how old they are).

The majority of Staten Island's Liberian immigrants are in low wage service or medical fields. They are struggling with illiteracy, have difficulty in finding employment, and poverty. The reputation of the Park Hill area for gang and drug violence has afflicted some Liberian youth, already victimized by the Civil War. Liberian youths caught up in criminal activity, if arrested as refugee status visa holders, they face deportation back to their homeland. Friction between the Liberians and local African-American community, over jobs, housing, and culture, has also been a source of tension for an already troubled community.

Why do we focus on the Muslim culture? All of this points toward a likely difficult period for America in this century. We will all encounter Islamic families with their own unique family rules and *incompatible Sharia laws*. Our Dependency Program has specific rules and methods for handling Native American culture cases. We now have to prepare for how we will specifically deal with Muslim citizens and their distinctive culture, which can be expected to conflict with Americas mixed culture and civil laws.

In terms of culture, Islam is more than a religion—*it is a way of life*. Spiritual beliefs and specific rules form equal parts of the Muslim faith, and no distinction exists between doctrine and laws, or the separation of church and state. No thought, act, contract, or relationship is beyond its scope. Christ's injunction to '*Render to Caesar the things that are Caesar's and to God the things that are Gods*' is alien to Islam. In fact, *it is the opposite.*

# CASE HISTORIES

**Florida: Deaths of Eight children put Hillsborough Kids Inc. in Limbo**

Source: John Barry, Times Staff Writer, *Tampa Bay Times* (abridged for this book)

"The homegrown, nonprofit agency charged with protecting 2,500 of Hillsborough County's most vulnerable children is at risk of losing its $65.5 million state contract because of eight dead kids. They died in the last two years while under the supervision of Hillsborough Kids Inc. ...

"The eight stood out in a Department of Children and Families [DCF] study of child deaths statewide. Seven of the eight children were under supervision because of reports of abuse, neglect or abandonment. DCF said no other agency in Florida had so many deaths. "... Among the most publicized: a 4-month-old boy who was beaten and thrown from a car on I-275. The ex-boyfriend of the baby's teenage mother was charged with his murder.

Another victim was a 5-month-old girl choked to death last year. Police charged her mother. Last year, an 18-month-old toddler ...wandered into the path of car in an apartment parking lot and killed. ...

"The two most common shortcomings identified by DCF: ***failures of frontline workers in the most potentially dangerous homes to understand the family dynamics, and failures of their supervisors*** *to give enough guidance.* DCF administrator Carroll says effective casework is based on common sense, intuition and experience as much as following checklists and completing questionnaires. Supervisors are key, especially when caseworkers are young. ...

"New software will flag families at high risk for abuse: those with teen mothers, day care problems, past domestic violence and parents who were abused as children. Most of the factors showed up in the eight deaths. The agency also has started a Family Finding program to identify biological or adoptive family members, teachers, coaches, and friends to form support teams for children."

**Why wasn't a *Guardian ad Litem* volunteer appointed to these cases?**

The purpose of the Guardian program—to be an independent and effective voice for the **Best Interest of the Children.** *Resource limitations are no excuse!*

**Perspective:** Readers should note that in comparison to states like California, New York, and Illinois, Florida (now the 4th largest state by population) is one of the better states, in terms of its *Guardian ad Litem* program effectiveness, with about 80% coverage for serious children's cases. Nevertheless, improvements and enhancements can make it better. We proposes areas for improvement for the sake of these **little voices.**

The following cases are from our private notes and from memory as Guardian ad Litem volunteers. **We did not use confidential files or any restricted information.**

The authors have produced *summaries* of selected cases that we hope would be both interesting as well as instructive. **We altered all names, gender, dates, and places to protect the children, the parents, and others, out of respect for their privacy.**

Our goal is to inform readers about the positive aspects of *Guardian ad Litem* Program and the Department of Children & Family (DCF), and to compare them (partly) to the challenges faced nationally. While we from time criticize DCF and ECA operations and management policies, our *principal goal* is to provide constructive ideas and positive solutions in order to make this a much better child support system. **One cannot find solutions by ignoring current weaknesses or masking problems.**

This book *frankly* discusses cases, provides a basis for a dialogue on future societal challenges, and offers solutions to America's ever-growing family crisis. Many individuals played vital roles in these cases. It really was a *"team effort."*

# THE SNAKE OIL CASE

The father of this beautiful nine-year old child was previously involved in criminal activities, such as domestic violence, pimping, selling and using illegal drugs and alcohol abuse. The mother was in jail for prostitution and selling drugs *in front of her child*. CPI sent the young girl to live with her grandfather, as the primary caregiver.

The father, Sam, was not present when mom had been caught doing prostitution and drugs. As a result, he escaped jail time. Nevertheless, Sam had drug abuse and other issues, and agreed to work his case plan over a timeframe of one year, if he wanted to reunite with his daughter. His case plan included being free of illegal drugs and alcohol, taking parenting classes, doing a psychosocial evaluation and recommended treatment, and providing proof he earned enough to support himself and his daughter.

Sam was a very troubled father. He had great difficulty getting off his alcohol and drug habits, but he tried. We interviewed him many times with his daughter. He seemed to be forever "selling himself," by boasting about his "born again Christian" beliefs and trying to bamboozle us about how he became hooked on drugs from an auto accident and the doctor's prescription pain pills, while avoiding the truth about his past criminal activities and serious booze history. This GAL labeled him, *"snake oil salesman."*

GAL interviewed dad and his daughter when we visited him, under supervision of Annie's aunt and uncle. A typical dialogue went as follows:

"Sam, how long have you lived here? What are the total monthly costs?"

"For many years now, I pay about $350 monthly."

"Can you be a little more specific?"

"Well, almost two years; my total monthly costs are about $1,200."

"Annie, how did you like it when you were living here?"

"She loves it here, *don't you Annie*?" Dad replied.

"Yes, it's really very nice!" She finally answered.

"Do you have any difficulties at home or in school?"

Again, dad responds: "She's *always happy* when Annie visits me; she's doing great at school, *right Annie*?"

One of the troubling issues during these interviews was that he frequently answered questions we asked his daughter; she was now 10 years old. At this point, I whisper to Miriam, my partner GAL, to take Annie outside, so they can have a more private dialogue *without* dad. I continued to talk to Sam.

Most of Sam's answers were bullshit! For example, he said, "everything is going great with his case plan tasks," when we knew he failed the last UA (urine analysis). "He said he writes to Annie's mom almost every day, and encourages his daughter to send letters to her mom."

Meanwhile, our interview with her mom in jail indicated that she "never received mail from her daughter." In addition, she said Sam "only calls her about once a month."

From now on, we decided to interview father and child *separately*, away from each other, to avoid the problem of him always answering for her. This seemed to work, especially at her school. As a result, we became very suspicious of Sam's real motives. Was child sex abuse involved here? Did he really love his daughter? Maybe he was mainly interested in the welfare funds he would get as the primary caregiver.

One day, our case coordinator summoned us—really me. Her director and the GAL attorney were also present at this *unexpected* crucial meeting. Something *very serious* has happened! Did I break the rules, again? After waiting for nearly a half hour outside their office, they called us into this somber meeting. "Show us proof or *evidence* that the father in your case is indeed a so-called *snake oil salesman*," the assistant director asked.

This characterization of the father was impossible for me to justify. I also stupidly put this portrayal of him in my email reports, which were marked "confidential." "Okay, I screwed up! I promise that I'll be much more careful in the future." (Miriam had warned me, but I did not follow her emphasis on "Political Correctness." We also did not realize that emails are *not confidential*. Defense lawyers can ask for them during discovery in future trials. GAL management accepted my *naive* admission and apology.

Mom in the jailhouse: Miriam was a bit nervous going into any jail. She had never experienced this before. Momma Sue said she really loved and missed her daughter. "I would love to have a recent picture of Annie."(We promised to get pictures).

Mom wrote to Annie many times, but the daughter did not get any of her letters. As a result, she did not write back. The father could be intercepting mom's letters. We decided to interview the grandfather and the aunt of the child, in order to obtain a little better insight and perspective as to the truth of this situation. Why the lack of contact?

The grandparents were frightened when we showed up at their door one weekend, with our Guardian Badges fully displayed. They thought we were the police, coming to take away their granddaughter. It took time to regain their confidence before Miriam and I could begin interviewing (we *never* exposed our official badges like that again).

One has to find out what really motivates people during interviews. Is it control over money? Is it a power play and control over the child? Could it be animosity towards one of the parents? What is their agenda? It was obvious that they were *totally against* Sam, their son-in-law, and father of Annie, married to their "abused" daughter, "Sue who was rotting in jail. He was the cause of all her problems," they claimed. "He's 'the John,' who sold their daughter's services, and led her into hard-drugs, and all that criminal stuff." Our Suzy was a victim of Sam's sleazy behavior," they angrily argued.

Upon further investigation, GAL learned more of the truth of the case, by talking to Annie's uncle, her schoolteachers, studying the historical record, and *most importantly*, directly speaking to her therapist. Daddy was clearly not innocent. We *instinctively* did not trust him. However, we cannot depend on human instincts alone; they do not count for evidence in any court of law. We gathered all the evidence we could, and then connected all the dots. We reviewed the father's therapy summary report; spoke to his relatives; and summarized all available documented facts for the next JR hearing.

In spite of our suspicions, we had to do **"What is in the Best Interest of the Child."**

Months later the father diligently worked his case plan. These GALs had no alternative but to agree with the CM, the Assistant DA, to recommend *reunification* of dad with his daughter to the judge. We had no right to keep parents from their child based in our "gut feelings." We remained guarded. We monitored this child's school development, weeks after she went north to her to dad's family home in NY. We interviewed the teachers and school counselors in NY by phone and e-mail. Finally, the case closed.

Thereafter, caseworkers in the NY area monitored the family for three additional months. After completing this case, verifying that the child was indeed happy living with dad, and there were no *known* sexual abuse problems with the father (we were *intuitively* concerned with possible sex abuse, because he pimped for her mom, but had no evidence).

It was extremely difficult for us to "*let go emotionally*," with our first case, after the Judge made his decision. We wondered how Annie is doing, today as a teenager. Did her scars from her troubled past heal? Did her mom re-establish the relationship with her child and the father? We also wondered how dad's "*snake oil sales*" were progressing.

**Lessons Learned:** Be careful about forming conclusions before you have investigated *all* the facts. Never label anyone! Any characterization of individuals can be used against us in court. We must not get too emotionally involved in cases; *you have to let go*. Instincts and "gut feelings" must be held in check, unless one finds evidence to confirm them. Once a case leaves the court's jurisdiction, GALs should expect to have a hard time controlling or inquiring about anything. Other states do not have to cooperate; they have their own enormous caseloads, and will not be bothered by calls and emails.

# CLUELESS CASE

Webster's dictionary defines clueless as "providing no clue, completely or hopelessly bewildered, unaware, ignorant, or foolish." This mother, whom we call, Mary Jane, fit this definition *perfectly*. She had been in and out of the legal system more than seven years. These Guardians were shocked by the size of her file, which consisted of numerous volumes that covered a complete ten-foot shelf.

Her case would close, and then reopen again, again, and again. It was a perfect pattern of a "revolving door" scenario. The case would open due to various problems between her husband (domestic violence) and the children. The innocent male child was absolutely beautiful. A second female child was born soon after we accepted this case. God gave them two wonderful gifts. *What will they do with His gifts?*

Mary Jane was a safety hazard, to herself and to her children. For example, she would leave the door unlocked and the child would wander out on to the streets alone. The other child had asthma, but mother continued to be a chain-smoker. Her house was a complete mess, unless we showed up by appointment; then she would quickly fix it up prior to our visitation. When GAL showed up unannounced (most of the time), we would find dirty clothes on the floor in the kitchen, garbage in the two bedrooms—*filth was everywhere*. Ashtrays were completely full, usually with a burning cigarette on the plastic couch. We would naturally inform her of the safety hazards to them and the children. She would promise to correct her ways—*until our next surprise visit.*

During GAL's next unannounced visit, we found leftover food on the stove, bugs crawling throughout this thousand square-foot apartment. In fact, the children had lice, and sent home from the school. Mary Jane claimed that they got it from the daycare school. *A clear case of denial* These GALs were anxious about sitting down on her furniture, in case we might catch something. (Parents may be very poor, but still keep their home clean; there is no excuse for lack of basic hygiene for your children).

Poor Mary Jane, this *clueless* mother, became very emotional, with flowing crocodile tears before the judge at every court hearing. Mary claimed she loved her children, but she had no idea how to be a *responsible parent*. She did not know the essentials about cleanliness. She was clueless about safety. Yes, her case plan required that she learn these *fundamental* parenting requirements, but she must have been sleeping during those courses, or she did not really understand a damn thing. GAL tried gently to guide her as much as we could, over a one-year period, to no avail.

This mother had a state provided lawyer, SSI funds, food stamps, free medical care, free Daycare, and we found a low cost bed for her children (paid for by a GAL's charity, Sun Coast for Children). We believed this couple was abusing the state system to get additional all kinds of free services, but GAL could not prove our assertion.

They were in and out of the court system for almost a decade. They knew more about the imperfect legal system than we knew; they especially knew about parental "legal rights." When she went to court for her required Judicial Reviewed (JR) every five months, she would get extremely emotional and began ranting. Once her court appointed attorney had to tell her "*just shut up and listen to the judge!*"

## ROBERT AND MIRIAM FERTIG

One late evening, at about 11 PM, Robert was suddenly awakened by a phone call from the police. "Are you the Guardian for Mary Jane?" the officer asked.

"Yeah, what's happening?"

"We got a call from someone that Mary Jane is screaming. Do you have her address? I will sent a squad to the home. Meet the officers there if you can."

I quickly got dressed and drove to Mary Jane's home. Police were waiting for me outside. After showing them my GAL badge, I asked, "What's the situation?"

"It was a false alarm," they said. "Mary Jane was watching a horror movie with her TV very loud. Her neighbor thought she was being battered."

I did a follow-up investigation. She was clearly intoxicated, and all smiles when she finally opened the door. "What are you doing here so late? Come in and have a drink."

This was a hopeless case, but these GALs had *no definitive* reasons to recommend Termination of Parental Rights (TPR). Mary Jane was married to John, but we rarely saw the husband because he worked nights, and was sleeping upstairs during the day. According to the neighbors, they often drank too much, had many loud arguments, which ultimate led to domestic violence (DV). However, the couple would do most of their case plan, clean up their act, and the case would close. A year or two later, DV and substance abuse would occur again, and they would be back in the court, and given another case plan. It was a typical example of "a revolving door" situation.

One day, our Guardian lawyer told us "Why don't you lighten up on these parents? "Give her some slack, so that we can close this case," he insisted.

"Did he ever visit these parents or their two children?" I asked. *"You know nothing about them!* Why don't you stick to your legal role and let us write our report for the court, *as we see it*? We are the observers of the facts; you are the legal expert—*right?"*

He was pissed at us, went over our heads and complained to higher management. *Surprise, it backfired!* Management agreed that he overstepped his legal role. "GAL is on the front lines and responsible for Visitation and JR reports," she said.

Later another attorney told us, "look this is the best that these parents can do for their children." We agree, but how much must we lower our standards?

After one year, with very little progress to report, we had no definitive evidence to support child neglect or abuse by these parents. *Being a clueless mom is not a crime.*

After completing their case plan, the case closed. It may re-open in the future, but that is not our concern. There are many clueless families out there, and some are worse off than Mary Jane's case. We have to look for what is possible. ***The ideal family does not exist!***

**Lessons Learned:** Do not expect to work miracles (leave that to God). Be realistic about your goals with families. The CM role is to provide all the necessary referrals to help parents. Do not measure the family environment by your own middle-class standards. Your primary goal is to focus on the safety and welfare of the children. Unfortunately, effective action is only taken by the court, *after* the children are injured or killed.

# DEFIANT TEEN CASE

*Life is really simple, but we insist on making it complicated.*
—Confucius

This was a Hispanic family with a cocaine-addicted daughter, that we will call Yolanda. She was involved with the wrong crowd in high school. They were undoubtedly negative role models. They were peer group gangs who sell drugs, and were sexually permissive. This teenager gave birth to a drug-addicted baby, from an unknown father.

Our young mother had a *defiant* attitude problem, when we first met her after taking on this case. The 17-year old mother of this infant child had a "big chip on her shoulder." Yolanda believed that she had certain "rights in America," such as, her right to have free sex, her right to do drugs, her right to a free attorney, and her right to do whatever else she damn well pleases. *"You can't tell me what to do!"* she said.

Yolanda was reluctant to do her case plan, which she knowingly accepted and signed. My spouse Miriam, spoke fluent Spanish as well as perfect English, and she tried to convince this young woman that she *did not* have all the "rights" that she thought she had. *"Your new born child also has a right to be drug-free!"* Miriam stated furiously.

Yolanda had a good family to back her up, and they were willing to put up with her crap because they really loved their baby granddaughter, even though she was born a bastard. They were one of those exceptional "integrated Hispanic Christian families."

After her many, many relapses on drugs, Yolanda finally realized that her family, who were also going through difficult financial times, loved her and the baby, and they would do whatever was required to support her and their grandchild. Yolanda had a choice: If she did not get her bullshit together, these grandparents would adopt her baby and kick her butt out of their home. (Tough love was required in this situation).

Finally, after many months of false starts and hassles, Yolanda began to yield some positive action. She completed most case plan tasks and started to listen to us GALs. She was also able to get a part-time job to support her child. Her drug abuse problem took many more months of therapy services, before she overcame her addiction.

In about one year, Yolanda reunified with her child. She became a "responsible parent." That was a clear success story for the child and for us GALs. We give credit primarily to God's grace, and Yolanda's family. (We were merely instruments of *His mercy and love*).

**Lessons Learned:** Many teen parents don't have a clue about parenting. They are usually immature, and need a lot of "hand-holding." Referral services on parenting is essential. However, a positive attitude is also necessary. Wherever possible involve the entire family, who can also provide backup support.

# LOST IN THE SYSTEM CASE

Two brothers were lost in the children's dependency system. They fell between the cracks of the system. The GAL program, over a period of about five years, lacked sufficient volunteers to assign someone to this case, until Ken and Keith were six and seven years old. These children bounced around in the foster care system, to and from their drug-abuse, violent parents.

They soon lived *permanently* with a seventy-six-year-old, very sick aunt. To make matters worse, the CMs in charge of the case changed *five times*. In addition, the doctor responsible for this case misdiagnosed the brothers. He prescribed the *wrong* psychotropic meds. This "professional" recently moved to another state.

After seeing the boys, checking out their environment, and interviewing the foster mom and dad, we later went to see their teachers and guidance counselors. Professional teachers are those who take a *genuine* interest in their students. They knew a great deal about the behavior of these brothers (more than the foster parents did). Feedback from the teachers did *not* agree with what foster parents, CM and others were telling us.

These GALs attempted to communicate directly with the *newly* appointed CM, the *new* psychologist and *new* therapist. After getting no reply from them from numerous phone messages, we sent an email to the CM, copying her management, our coordinator, and finally got a response. "Why were they *all new* medical professionals?" we asked. The previous CM and doctor left *abruptly* for "unknown reasons," we were informed. We later learned that she wasn't paid due to budget problems. No pay, no service was her "professional answer."

Meanwhile, the foster parents were *demanding* medical services for about six months, to no avail. After a few visitation reports and emails, again copying the management in the chain of command, we finally got some action for these kids and their foster parents. Later we interviewed the sick aunt, the teacher, and the biological mom and dad.

## Interview with the Aunt

"Cathy, when did you step-in to care for these children?"

"Three years ago, my husband and I took responsibility for the boys, because of violence and drug addiction problems with my niece and her husband."

"When did you see them last?"

"I last met with them for their birthday." (She sees them monthly).

"Did you receive any financial or emotional support from their parents?

"None from the father! He told me he would not pay any costs for the children. (To date the father has not provided any support). Mother provides clothes, and some food."

These GALs later learned that the boy's late Grandmother opened a Trust Fund for them. (Could this be the significant motivating factor for the father's desire to get the boys under his control?)

"What was it like caring for these two children with your health issues?"

"The children were very active, difficult to control, but I loved them dearly."

"The biological father claims that, you are the cause for all their problems. What's your reaction?"

"He blames everyone, except himself. I believe he is Schizophrenic. The father goes to the 'The Hood' to get his drugs."

"According to CPI, there has been ten years of domestic violence between them (the parents). Why is your niece in jail, while her husband is free?"

"She got caught stealing; she broke probation. He escaped detection."

"The children are doing great in the foster care. They seem happy."

Aunt Cathy was extremely pleased.

"If your niece loves her boys, why doesn't she do what's best for them?"

"She absolutely loves them. She might be able to do her new case plan."

## Teacher Interview

Children's Name: Ken (DOB: 06/29/06), and Keith (DOB: 07/16/07)
Date and time of visit: 05/20/12 (follow-up school visit)
Location of visit: (please select one): Elementary School.
Name of caregivers, or foster parents: Joe and Ann.
Names of the Schoolteacher: Teresa and Sherry

GAL visited the children's school to gain a better understanding and a greater perspective of the situation and to obtain another viewpoint on the brothers' academic, emotional, social, and behavioral issues. We also interviewed each of the children separately, and spoke to their respective teachers, Teresa, Sherry, and Molly, the Director. Our direct observations follow:

**GAL Assessment:** Ken (6 yrs.), is communicative, the opposite of his brother Keith.

**Academically:** Ken is an "A" student, who excels in reading, but struggles with writing.

**Emotionally:** He is attached and bonds with the teacher; e.g., he frequently needs to hold the teacher's hand. He wants to please adults.

**Socially:** Ken is generally friendly with other peer students, teachers and adults.

**Observations:** During the last two weeks the child has been less engaged in class, needs more attention from teacher, is less focused, and is more outspoken. He was afraid to read his poem on home life in class (why is that so?)

Keith's (5 yrs.) teacher, Sherry, agrees with GALs observations that he is "very shy" and has very little eye contact with adults when we are talking to him.

**Academically:** Keith is a "B" student, who really excels in reading and math.

**Socially:** Keith seems to play the role of "the leader," and does not accept any directions from anyone. After his new psychotropic meds, Keith improved significantly, in terms of socializing.

**Observations:** He has aggressive problems, such as not following directions, shouting out, and fighting with his peers.

**Behavioral Problems:** He was suspended for various behavioral issues, and is only in first grade. Keith continues to see the school counselor weekly in peer group sessions.

**Foster Parents Interview:** When Miriam asked about discipline, foster parents Joe and Ann promptly replied, "Discipline at this home is mostly time-outs. Infractions include not eating all their food, not cleaning their room, and not following our rules."

Both children claimed they loved their foster parents. However, Keith often fights and yells at Ken. Keith also had a difficult time expressing himself. In contrast, his brother was very expressive. Both children seemed to be "guarded in responding to all GAL questions," especially Keith, who often said, "I don't remember."

**GAL Concerns:** The teachers and the school nurse should have known that the children are on psychotropic medications. The foster parents did not visit or talk to the children's teachers enough. Have the foster parents informed the psychologist *specifically* about the children's issues, at home and in school? If not, why not? Why is Keith so difficult, while Ken seems to be less problematic? Are these psychological and emotional issues? The professional doctors and therapists did not asked us about these children's issues. How can a psychologist and therapist do a professional job in *a damn vacuum*?

## Visitation Notes

Did we see child's sleeping area? Yes. All three children share the same bedroom.

Had a tour of home? Yes (required at initial visit)

Any concerns with the current placement? If so, what are they? It was a reasonably clean and safe environment. However, many "R-rated" violent electronic games, and TV programs could seriously affect their social interaction (see the appendix study).

Are the children on any medication? Yes (see attached medical report for specifics)

At the next meeting, it would be most important for us GALs to know if the brothers are truly happy. Do they have problems adapting to the new situations, and the changed environment? Are they are getting the essential therapy and psychotropic meds? They are about to be adopted, and these GALs wanted to be certain, *absolutely convinced* that it would be the best final placement for "our boys."

## GAL Recommendations

**Placement:** Both children should remain in their current placements. Any disruption of their current placement and environment could cause psychological or emotional harm.

**Visitations:** Mom remains incarcerated until spring, next year and dad visitations to his two children have been *essentially zero.*

**Permanency:** Based on available records that GAL reviewed, and our visitations, these Guardians currently agree with the State and CMs *new goal* of Adoption for both children, due to our direct investigation and observations over the past 12 months:

(1) There is no evidence of the children bonding with their biological parents.
(2) The parents have multiple charges pending for illegal drugs and domestic violence.
(3) The parents represent safety and welfare concerns because of drugs and DV.
(4) Both children absolutely need physical support and emotional permanency.
(5) Parents have not done their case plans, although given many opportunities to do so.

**Children Wishes:** Both children are too young to express their wishes fully.

**Timeline to permanency:** Shelter(s) Date: Removal 07/08/12.
**Adjudication of Dependency Date:** 09/16/12
**Current Case Plan Acceptance Date:** 10/02/12

## Children's status

**Mental/Medical Health:** Foster parents told GAL: "the prior CM (her supervisor is Jane), was *completely unresponsive* to foster parents many requests for psychological evaluation and counseling for the children." (This CM is no longer with ECA). "The new CM is a bit more responsive, "according to the foster mom and dad.

**Education/Daycare:** Both children enrolled in local elementary school. According to teachers and supervisor, the children are cooperative, *after* their new medications.

**Contacts with Parents:** GAL contacted the mother in jail, the teachers of children, the school counselor, the foster parents, the aunt, and we attempted to contact the father. GAL left phone messages five times with the father, and four times with the children's therapist and psychiatrist. Both professionals finally called GAL last week.

**Visitations:** The mother and father have visited the children infrequently at best.

**Placements:** Both brothers are now 14 months at the same Foster Care Home.

**Services needed for the Children:** These children appear to be well cared for, but they have special needs. Both are seeing another *new therapist*.

**Compliance with Case Plan:** Last Case Plan Goals, Adoption, with Reunification as a secondary goal; these tasks were approved by the court on 09/04/12.

1. **Mother's Progress with Case Plan Tasks:**
   PAR Substance Abuse Evaluation: **Noncompliant.**
   Couples Counseling: **Noncompliant.**
   Psycho Evaluation: **Noncompliant.**
   Random urine drops: **Noncompliant.**
   Income and housing: **Compliant.**
   PAR parenting classes: **Noncompliant**

2. **Father's Progress with Case Plan Tasks:**
   PAR substance abuse evaluation: **Noncompliant.**
   Couples Counseling: **Noncompliant.**
   Psycho Evaluation: **Noncompliant.**
   Random urine drops: **Noncompliant.**
   Income and housing: **Compliant.**
   PAR parenting classes: **Noncompliant**

## Summary/Assessment

Mother is *NOT* actively working on her case plan. She will be released soon.

Father is *NOT* actively working on his case plan. He is *NOT* cooperating with GAL.

GAL learned that *qualified* foster parents want to adopt both children, after the TPR trial and final decision by the court. The potential adopting parents did not understand why the biological parents have *another* opportunity to complete yet one more case plan. We explained that the judge is required to give *all parents* every opportunity before TPR.

**Respectfully submitted by Robert & Miriam Fertig, M.A.**

This was a "no-brainer" TPR case, since the biological parents did not do their case plans; they did not visit their children enough or provide meaningful support; and domestic violence and drug abuse continued for years. Nevertheless, no TPR trial is easy. We had to *again* study the complete file and produce an extremely detailed report (see the appendix for a typical example of a representative TPR report).

Miriam acted as "defense lawyer," during rehearsals, as Robert would be in the "hot" witness chair, for the trial.

The group did an excellent job and stuck to the facts of the case. It was really a team effort. Months later, we received notice that our side won the case for the **Best Interest of the children.** They now have an *opportunity* to live a "normal life."

These GALs, thank God, stayed officially connected with the case until adoption. As the New Orleans expression goes, **"It's not over, until the fat lady sings."**

## Therapy or Psychotropic Drugs?

The co-authors of a 20-year-old study promoting the use of prescription drugs to combat the effects of attention deficit hyperactivity disorder (ADHD) are now claiming the report may have overstated medication's benefits.

According to a report in the *New York Times*, at least two co-authors of the highly influential study – called the Multimodal Treatment Study of Children with ADHD – have come forward to express concern that the original report also downplayed the benefits of behavioral therapy.

*"There was lost opportunity to give kids the advantage of both and develop more resources in schools to support the child—that value was dismissed,"* said co-author Dr. Gene Arnold, a child psychiatrist and professor at Ohio State University.

*"I hope it didn't do irreparable damage,"* added a second co-author, Dr. Lilly Hechtman of Montreal's McGill University. **"The people who pay the price in the end is the kids. That's the biggest tragedy in all of this."**

The report originally claimed that not only was medication like Adderall and Ritalin more effective than therapy, but also that combining the two treatments offered little to no benefit to the patient. Even a 2001 report that showed a combination of medication and therapy effectively treating ADHD symptoms by 12 percent over medication only (68 – 56 percent) labeled the results *"small by conventional standards."*

Boosted by marketing from pharmaceuticals, prescriptions for ADHD drugs have skyrocketed since the early 1990s, alongside a significant rise in the diagnosis of ADHD in general.

According to new data from the Centers for Disease Control and Prevention, 15 percent of high-school-age children were diagnosed with this disorder, with roughly 3.5 million currently taking medication. These numbers stand in stark contrast to the 600,000 or so children diagnosed with ADHD in 1990.

*"The numbers make it look like an epidemic. Well, it's not. It's preposterous,"* Keith Conners, a psychologist and professor emeritus at Duke University, said to the Times earlier in December. *"This is a concoction to justify the giving out of medication at unprecedented and unjustifiable levels."*

One of the reasons medication has been used so often to treat the disorder is that, at the cost of $200 a year, it is significantly cheaper than therapy, which can run up to $1,000 a year or more and is not covered as comprehensively by insurance companies. While medication can be helpful, it also has its consequences – potential addiction, anxiety, depression, insomnia and, in some cases, suicidal tendencies and hallucinations.

Behavioral therapy, meanwhile, focuses on developing a child's long-term academic and social skills. According to psychologist Ruth Hughes of the advocacy group Children and Adults with Attention-Deficit/Hyperactivity Disorder, medication may make a child ready to learn important skills, but it still requires someone to teach them.

Now, new studies are suggesting that the effects of medication begin to decrease once a child grows older, suggesting it is extremely difficult to calculate how a child will react as they reach young adulthood. Some researchers pin the blame on the fact that many children stop taking the pills, while others say it demonstrates the inability of a medication-only approach to conclusively treat the disorder.

"My belief based on the science is that symptom reduction is a good thing, but adding skill-building is a better thing," Stephen Hinshaw, a psychologist at the University of California, Berkeley, said to the Times. "If you don't provide skills-based training, you're doing the kid a disservice. I wish we had had a fairer test."

Lessons Learned: GALs should never give up, *especially* when safety and welfare become clearly a major issue. Some parents are less educated and may be "clueless" about basic parenting. Be patient and find available services within state sources to help them. Know the limits of your capabilities: what you are equipped to do from your education and experiences, and *most importantly*, what you cannot handle. GALs cannot seek TPR just because a parent is ignorant of parenting. Parents should have every opportunity to complete their case plan tasks. The case is not over until the judge makes a decision, and final appeal. Good, detailed record keeping is essential to win a case for your children. GALs need sufficient knowledge about meds and their possible side effects. Many good public and private sources are available to help children and their parents.

# PATTERN OF DENIAL CASE

Martin stated on our first visit to his home, *"I didn't do anything wrong."* He was a good loving father who provided everything for his boy, Johnny. "The mother was the real problem! She is the violent drug addict, not me. Why did the police (CPI) take my boy away? They had no damn right to take him from me!"

Our first meeting with the father was in his bug infested, filthy shack of a home. We immediately moved our interview outside, since Miriam was choking from cigarette smoke and bitten by fleas and other bugs. I got the anti-bug lotion from my car.

This dad was a *non-stop* talker. I had to interrupt him many times to ask important questions; otherwise, the visit would be a total waste.

"How did Johnny come into this world?"

"We had a party one night, and his drunken mother jumped on me."

"So you had nothing to do with this sexual encounter?"

"Well, she took advantage of me when I was slightly under the influence."

"Isn't it true that, from this beer party, your beautiful boy was conceived?"

"Yes, he's beautiful—and extremely intelligent boy."

"I understand from your file that you say, "Mom beat you up. Is that correct?"

"That's right! She also took a kitchen knife and cut my belly."

"Why don't you pull up your shirt and show us your old wounds." He pulled up the shirt. *Nothing was visible.* "How could a woman attack a strong man like you?"

"Well, she first hit me with a bottle, when I wasn't looking."

"Both of you were drinking, right?"

"Yeah, we had a few beers. She can't handle more than two beers."

"Why don't you fix up this place and make it safer for your child?"

Martin became extremely indignant. *"My place is safe!* Are you blind? Can't you see I'm working on improving this place?"

There was no sense debating him about his unsafe house. *He was in complete denial!* Before leaving, I asked permission to take pictures of "his countless improvements." He allowed it. My cell phone photos gathered clear evidence of safety and health issues, for discussion with the CM, GAL management, and I would present them at the next JR.

Next, we went on to see the mother. Dolly was more cooperative, although she was angry and did not trust ECA, the CM, or the court dependency system. "Those CM assholes couldn't keep their records accurate," she claimed. "I did whatever they asked me to do, and they keep asking for more stuff, delaying reunification with my son."

We were the third GAL, and she had to deal also with the fourth CM on her case. Her house was safer and cleaner, however. A summary of our formal visit notes follows:

**Mother's Visitation Report:**

**Children's Name:** *Johnny (DOB XX/XX/XX)*

**Date and time of visit:** *July (Friday 10-11:00 AM)*

Location of visit: *Mother's Home.*

Name of caregiver/foster parent: *Dolly Parton*

Name of adult(s) living in the home: *Dolly & paramour, Bob*

Name of person conducting visit: *Robert & Miriam Fertig*

Has the child's placement changed since your last visit? *No*

How did the child appear? *He was clean, happy, bonding (he wanted mom to pick him up frequently). He has toys & clothes. He likes to drink juice. Mom avoids sweets.*

Did you see child's sleeping area? *Yes, he sleeps on couch (child needs a youth bed)*

Had tour of home? *Yes. We did not observed any health or safety hazards*

Any concerns with the current placement? If so, what are they? *None at mother's home*

Is the child on any medication? *None known at this time. However, he was coughing.*

If yes, what is the name of the medication and the dosage? (You should request to see the medication and get this information directly from the container): *If yes, you must notify your volunteer supervisor and/or GAL attorney

Is there information about the child the court should know? *He was great at foster care.*

Does the child want to attend court? *No! He has lung issues; do not expose him to others.*

Where is the child attending school/daycare? *Grace Daycare*

Is the child in special classes? *N/A*

Are there any services the child needs? (i.e., medical, therapeutic, educational)

If yes, what are they? *None known.*

Does the child have any other needs? *He needs lots of TLC.*

Are the children visiting with their parents? *Yes, 2-4 hour visits weekly, unsupervised.*

How is visitation going? *She missed three visits due to her recent auto accident.*

Any other information you feel is important: *The child has been with foster care since Oct. CM has delayed Home Study for inconsequential reasons.*

1. Due to failure to pay child support, the father had been arrested for DWLSR and Domestic Battery against mother in YY/YY. His criminal case is pending. He admitted that he beat her on YY/YY. Mother said she is "scared" of him. A court restraining order is currently active.
2. Mother has completed her case plan. All swabs were negative in XX/XX, except one. She claims it was a "false positive."
3. GAL believes a "bias" for the father (against the mother) by the new CM. The CM accepts the "word of father" without

verification. Dad claims income of $2,000/month *without* proof; he was trusted to correct home safety problems; and he did not complete required AAA meetings after only two sessions.
4. Mother receives food stamps. She is looking for work. Currently her paramour Bob financially supports her. GAL is not sure how long this will last.
5. We recommend overnights for mother, since we verified that most of her case plan tasks were done and bonding exists between child and mom.

After learning of our report to the court, the father began threatened us during follow-up visitations. His rage became more serious during our last unannounced visit, when we saw that his kitchen cabinets were unlocked and contained dangerous chemicals, plastic bags, and knives that this active child would certainly play with. The fourth CM on this case was frustrated when he tagged along with us at visitations, especially when we pointed-out obvious safety and health hazards.

After an "Advocacy Meeting," which we requested, GAL management decided, for safety reasons, to replace us with GAL David, a big strong retired police officer. While I was reluctant to allow the father to intimidate us, Miriam's exposure was my major concern. We passed our files to David. He would be handling this "challenging" case.

**Lessons learned:** Once the relationship with a parent comes into conflict, it is difficult to observe them with their children. Do not ever expose yourself to potential danger. If the child is in imminent or actual danger, document the reasons why, and do whatever it takes to get action from supervisors and the court. Nothing is, as it seems. GALs must *"Look under all the rocks"* to find the factual deceptions and falsehoods.

# MENTALLY CHALLENGED CASE

Our most tragic case was a mentally challenged young mother, in her early twenties. Martha's doctor diagnosed her as both bipolar and schizophrenic. She was a danger to herself as well as to her newborn child. After she gave birth to Sally, hospital staff had to fight paramour Charley, the father, in order to take the baby away from them.

The key problem with mother was that she stayed off her meds weeks before giving birth, in order to ensure that the baby not be affected by her prescription drugs. Though staying off her medication for such a long time caused her to be extremely nervous and easily upset, after birthing. The mother *really* loved her new baby but she did not understand the basic rudiments of caring for her newborn infant daughter. Charley was a proud but hopeless dad, trying to care for his first child as well. It was a classic case of mentally challenged parents. They did not know a damn thing about parenting.

These GALs selected the case shortly after the court decided to remove infant Sally to the paternal aunt, Susan. We attended the first CM Staffing meeting with the mother, the father, the aunt, and two "expert" ECA supervisors were present. They formally presented the plan using flip charts, at the initial meeting with the parents. I thought we were at a damn business meeting. We had already reviewed the complete history of the case and knew that mom was mentally challenged. Dad was unpredictable as well.

We sat silently as the supervisor went over the case plan in every detail. We did not understand how CM staff could present a plan that was *assured to fail*. The parents were required to: attend parenting classes (an essential task); have random urine analysis (UAs) to test for alcohol and illegal drug usage; have proof of sufficient legal income to support the family; a psychological examination for mom; a psychosocial examination for dad; and finally, avoid any new criminal activities. These were "typical legal" court required tasks, but the parents did not understand shit, and they clearly would not do hese tasks anyway. We, and the aunt, went away from the meeting, *completely perplexed*.

Aunt Susan became the *temporary* relative caregiver for Sally, and we visited the child with the aunt and parents monthly. During the following year, GAL monitored and investigated everything to do with this case. We observed that Martha could not care for her infant; she would become extremely upset when the baby cried; she would wash her hands and arms 4-5 times after the baby pooped. Once she stuck her fingers down Sally's throat when she seemed to be choking on food. We stopped her just in time. It was a sad *and* scary scene to observe. This beautiful, twenty-something young mother also became extremely jealous of the aunt's control over "her baby."

As anticipated, both parents *did not* complete their case plans. Dad became more and more irate at each Staffing meeting, and at the court hearings to review their progress. Martha was a *certified schizophrenic*. She also had recent accidents while driving her car. (Why the state gives a driver's license to severely mentally challenged people is beyond our understanding). This mom would frequently *not* take her meds on a timely basis. She would often leave the stove on, burning the food, which could cause a fire. When we asked her a question, she would stare into space. She was in her own dream world, *far away from reality*. Martha was a clear danger to herself and her child.

## Summary/Assessment

GAL believes, after observing them for about one year, both Mother and Father represent probable risks for the child's safety and welfare, at this time. Mother and father do not have the skills or financial means of caring for their child. Interestingly, the father also later stated *he agrees* with GAL's current assessment.

We observed that the mother acted oblivious of her circumstances. On one occasion, the mother got upset when the child had a bowel movement. Father also acted angry and nervous when the child cried. Both parents lacked basic parenting skills, even though they took the required parenting course. Were they both sleeping, or is this course worthless?

Domestic violence (DV) has occurred between mom and dad. Recent outbursts between them at staffing meetings, *appears to confirm serious* incompatibility between them. The paternal aunt provides the child with a safe, secure and loving environment. GAL believes both mom and dad have psychological and emotional issues, based on the following direct investigation, our observations and documented evidence:

(a) Mother acts unstable; e.g., stares into space. Her answers were very abrupt.

(b) Father acts defensive, aggressive, especially when confronted by frequent Police calls to the home, and to other family members. He appears confused, is aggressive when he plays with his baby (pulling the baby from the crib without bracing his head).

(c) The apartment staff interviewed said that a neighbor complained that the father was abusive to the mom. Police found mom rolling in mud, completely naked.

(d) The father was observed drinking alcohol. GAL saw opened bottles, when visiting him unannounced. He was hung-over the night after seeing his child. Father claims, "He does not have *any* drinking problem."

(e) Father stated, "He is very pleased with his aunt's care of his child," at the staffing. "He wants his daughter to remain in the care of the aunt on a long term basis. He acknowledged that his girlfriend (mom) is unable to care for 'his' child."

(f) Mom stated she feels "cut-off from her child." She feels the aunt is over-controlling. (She has to be controlling for the safety and welfare of the infant).

(g) GAL & CM have no proof that father has sufficient legal income to support his family. He seems to depend on mom's government SSD payments for the bills.

(h) A police report stated that mom said, "He always hits her and is abusive." (Mom is afraid he might restrict her from her child if she filed an official complaint).

(i) Father said that he "wants to leave mother."

(j) Based on father's current behavior, GAL requests a Court Order that Psychological Evaluation and Anger Management be added to the father's Case Plan. GAL believes that these issues could seriously affect the child's safety and welfare.

**Respectfully Submitted, Robert & Miriam Fertig (GALs)**

Finally, months later, the court granted "Permanent Caregiver" status to the child's aunt. The father retained the right to petition the court to get his kid back, whenever he completes a case plan and finds a new mother who knows how to care for his child.

GAL questions: How can the state allow a man to have sex with a mentally challenged adult woman who does not know how to defend herself? Martha became a "ward of the state, yet one year later she gave birth to second child. This tragic story continues. New laws should be considered to protect adults who are mentally challenged.

**Lessons Learned:** The safety and welfare of the child is of critical importance. Gather evidence from as many sources as possible, and then connect all the dots. Mentally challenged parents continue to have rights to their child, *if* they take their meds as required, and *if* someone responsible makes sure that they do it. A relative who is more qualified can be a good alternative solution for permanency.

# TOUGH LOVE CASE

*True love by its nature, is uncompromising; it is freeing of self from selfishness and egotism. Real love uses freedom to attach itself unchangeably to another. In love, there is perfect freedom and yet one important limitation that preserves that love; that is the refusal to hurt the beloved.*

Events in the lives of this particular case were both tragic *and* magnificent. It was the case of two half-sisters from a young mother, Janus, with *two different fathers.* June was three-years old, and Peggy was eight. They were half-sisters. Janus, the younger mother of the two children was living with her "new paramour;" the state's terminology for "lovers" who avoid marriage commitments. They often do not take responsibility for what "free sex" produced—*God's very precious gift*, innocent children.

Janus had a previous paramour, namely Jack, who was the father of Peggy, the older child. Jack finally left this former girlfriend, got married to a RN, and was able to "get his act together" and complete his case plan. We came into the case when he was about 50% finished with his tasks. Our first act was to visit the parents and children.

We showed up at this poor-looking home in an average neighborhood. I knocked at the creaky door, and instantly heard multiple dogs barking (darn it, I left my pepper spray in the car). This strange looking character, about 75-years-old, suddenly appears from the garage and says, "What are you selling? Whatever the hell it is, we don't want it."

He had tattoos all over his body and a Hartley motorcycle in the garage. After we showed him our Guardian badges, he immediately welcomed us into the home. We presented our legal documents, signed by the judge. The grandfather of Peggy somehow knew what we were all about, became friendlier and introduced us to his son, Jack, the father of 8-year old Peggy, who was still working on his case plan.

Jack introduced us to his older father and mother-in-law, and his other teenage daughter, who was also living in this small meager home. We could smell chicken soup cooking on the stove. Here was an *extremely poor* family of seven that seemed to be very happy and content (Miriam found that when she was teaching in rich Greenwich, CT., that wealthy families were generally unhappy, discontent and many had psychological problems).

We asked daughter Peggy, what do you like to do? She said, "I like to go with my sister to McDonald's, when daddy can afford it, about once a month."

What would you like to be when you grow-up? "A bone doctor," she answered.

The teenager and her younger sister went into their bedroom to have a private conversation with GAL Miriam (women's talk). I stayed in the living room and interviewed the rest of the family, primarily the new mom of Peggy. Jack, the father of this wonderful child, said that he recently married this nurse, and she helped him greatly with his case plan tasks. What a loving, yet very poor family, I concluded.

Many families that we visited had "too much of everything," *except real love*! What is real love? In this case, it was giving to each member of the family whatever was required. It was sharing chicken soup together, as the main dinner meal. It was caring for the sick grandmother, in their home (and not putting her in some kind of Assisted-Living impersonal home or Hospice), and never asking, "why us, why should we be responsible?" There was an atmosphere in this home that seemed to express what *true love* is all about, within and between all the family members.

After about six months, this father completed his case plan in record time, and these GALs had no problem recommending reunification and final closure of his case.

Later we went to visit the young mother of the half-sisters, and finally saw her three-year old daughter, June. *What a contrast!* Janus, the young mother of the child was still living with her twenty-something paramour, Martin. They had serious addiction problems; they were living from place to place, with drug addicted "friends." This very young 3-year old child was dependent on mom; she was living with her on someone's bug-infested couch, moving from place to place; living the *life of a vagabond*. They could not get their life together. "The legal system was stacked against us," Martin claimed.

"That's the wrong attitude," Miriam replied. "The court sent us to help you care for your beautiful innocent child. This child is not getting basic fundamental care, like security, proper food, clean clothing, and health care."

These out-of-control addicts were incapable of providing their young daughter with the essentials. It was a disaster waiting to happen! GAL could not recommend reunification under these unsafe, unhealthy conditions. Janus knew that the judge would eventually take her child from her, and she cried "real tears of a mother who truly loved her baby," when informed that this was the *probable* outcome of their case.

Nonetheless, the Lord in *His mercy and love* sent us a perfect solution: Aunt Alice stepped into the case, at this *crucial last moment*, and she volunteered to take responsibility for her niece's child, and to become the *primary caregiver*.

Miriam and I spoke to the crying mother of June, outside of the courtroom. We spoke to her warmly, face-to-face: "We can see that you *really love* your daughter, so you must do what is best for her, right?" She did not answer.

"Well, what is the best for your baby girl, *at this time*? You certainly want her to grow up to be safe, healthy, and have a real home, don't you?"

Finally, she answered, yes.

"Okay, when you and your paramour 'get your act together' in the future you can appeal to the court to get your daughter back. Permanent guardianship does *NOT* mean *permanent*!" We explained that the only thing permanent is that the aunt had full legal responsibility for the child, *until* the court decides to reunite the biological parents.

The CM agreed with our definition and assured her that was the truth: "As your child grows-up with your aunt, you can also see her whenever you want, under supervision of your aunt."

Mom and dad decided to give up their precious little girl, for the good of their child's future welfare. ***It was a perfect case of tough love!***

**Lessons Learned:** Never judge a book by its cover: Poor families are often more caring families; they are usually better Christians, as well. Sometimes addicts have to "crash" before they are ready for professional help. Do not jump to conclusions, until you gather and study *all* the facts of the case. If you fully understand the problem, you then just might find a reasonable solution.

# BABY MACHINE CASE

"Some mothers are like bunny rabbits," the judge (who shall remain nameless) said at a recent conference. However, rabbits know instinctively when to not reproduce. When food is scarce, they automatically stop reproducing. Theresa Jones and Rob Wassermann were "paramours," those who live together without any marriage commitments to each other, and then frequently have unprotected sex. Both parents had an infant boy and previous eighteen-month girl. Both parents were known cocaine sellers and users, during the past five years, according to their file.

Miss Jones was released from jail early, to give birth at the Halfway House. The *crack-addicted baby* was born soon thereafter. GAL visited the mother at her apartment. Our first impressions were that she was young, attractive, dressed properly, and articulate. She prepared a special room for her newborn baby boy, filled with crib and toys, when her baby comes home from the hospital. We introduced ourselves by stating that our goal is *primarily her children*. We want to help reunite her with the children. We gave mom our business card. "Please call us if you have any questions," Miriam declared.

After studying the Jones and Wassermann file, we realized that "first impressions," might not be that relevant in this case. Miss Jones had a *very long* criminal record. She was also convicted in a previous TPR trial, some years ago. Another family later adopted her three earlier children. We create a "timeline" for all of more serious cases. Here is a brief sample of their case timeline:

**Time-Line of Significant Parental Events** (abbreviated for this book):

## Date Events

| | |
|---|---|
| 5/14/10 | Theresa Jones incarcerated for illegal drug usage. |
| 8/30/10 | Jones gives birth to David after release from confinement. Child David sent to Children's Hospital due to withdrawal problems at birth. |
| 10/22/10 | We Visited child David at the Medical Foster Care home. Observation: Infant David had tremors. He needs special meds and diet. |
| 11/18/10 | Received signed releases from mom (dad signed one week later). |
| 11/21/10 | Visited child David with mom and foster care mom at Help-A-Child. |
| 12/12/10 | Called foster mom to inquire about David. Mom missed two meetings with David, without any calls or valid excuses. |
| 12/15/10 | The first JR, with goal of Reunification or Permanent Guardianship. |
| 01/25/11 | Visited David at Medical Foster Care home (see GAL trip report). |
| 1/28/11 | Attended medical staffing for David. All agreed that David was progressing, but had special medical needs. |
| 3/14/11 | Visited David at Children's Med. Services. Both parents were present. Parents were playing with baby. (It was an artificial "fishbowl" situation). |
| 3/18/11 | Called Theresa Jones twice, left messages. |

| | |
|---|---|
| 4/07/11 | GAL disputes Staffing report about Mr. Wassaman: dad claims he's working but had no proof of $700 cash funds. Could this be drug money? Staffing did not care about his source of money; "that's not our concern." |
| 4/11/11 | Visited Mr. Wassaman & Theresa Jones. Both acted strange. They were burning candles during daylight (we suspect they were smoking pot). |
| 4/14/11 | GAL is *against* unsupervised visits. Case plans are only 50% completed.<br><br>We object, but the judge grants reunification, effective in 30 days. |
| 4/20/11 | We visited little David at Day Care center. We noticed a significant improvement. The child is now socializing with other children. |
| 5/11/11 | Medical Foster Mom calls GAL regarding problem with parent's failure to pick up child: *"Something strange going on with parents."* GAL tells her, *"Do not drop off children."* CM later agrees with our recommendation. |
| 5/15/11 | CM informs GAL both parents UAs tested positive for Cocaine. |
| 7/21/11 | GAL attempted to visit parents. Manager says they were evicted still owing $1,800 in back rent. They moved to a local motel. |

**Summary of Parental Behaviors:**
- Theresa Jones had prior TPR's, in 2009 (see attached court records).
- Both Theresa Jones and Mr. Wassaman have new criminal records selling illegal drugs, theft, etc. (see attached official police and court records).
- Both parents failed to keep scheduled appointments with CM, GAL & Medical Foster Care mom, numerous times, without any return calls or valid excuses.

- Bonding between parents and children does not exist; child screams constantly.
- GAL believes that both parents were not truthful.
- Both parents do not have legal income to support themselves and their children.
- Both parent's UAs were positive for cocaine (again, they relapsed).
- Both parents have failed to cooperate with GAL.
- Parents did not complete case plans, although given opportunities to do so.
- GAL concludes parents are a danger to the safety and welfare of their children.

After various court motions and defense lawyer delays, the case ultimately closed with Termination of Parental Rights (see Appendix on TPR). The case closed successfully, but these GALs, months later, found out that the mother gave birth to another *premature addicted baby*. She sold the infant to a childless couple. It was a "private contract." GALs had no right to inquire about the new infant's condition. Two TPR's, all successfully adopted, but one addicted infant was sold to a desperate childless family.

**Lessons Learned:** Remember that GALs focus is about the children. CMs focus is the parent's case plan. Establish a good relationship with the CM, but do not inform her about your "views of the case." Sometimes nothing is, as it seems. Some parents will lie, steal and cheat to get whatever they desire. If one wants to find the whole truth, you have to be prepared to look under rocks. Parents cannot change established bad habits, especially substance abuse, in just a few months. *That is completely unrealistic!*

# TROUBLED LAKE CASE

These were two different cases, involving four children, in the same area. One set of babies lived with the caregiver in a region of Florida called "Troubled Lake." The other older children lived about 10 miles south of their sisters, in a good foster caregiver's family home. We were committed to visit the girls and their pending new parents, after a successful TPR, during the adoption phase, which was now in the works.

We heard from another GAL, that a woman ran out of gas in the Troubled Lake, and went to get help. She came back with the tow truck. Shockingly, she found her car sitting on four cinder blocks—all four wheels were missing.

That was the kind of neighborhood we were about to encounter. It is an area of shacks, known for drugs and violence. One should never go there at night, without some means of protection. Being fearless, GAL Robert said to his spouse Miriam, "that's, *just a good fairy-tale*. Besides, I have my million-volt Teaser, if any problems should crop up."

We looked for the home for about half an hour, but could not find it. Suddenly we saw a street sign on a dirt road with *huge* potholes. Miriam said, *"Let's get the hell out of here!"*

I decided that we had gone over 40 miles; and we might as well go the extra mile. A slow ride down the extremely bumpy road finally led us to the home. A sign read, *"Beware of Dog."* All at once, this big man with a huge potbelly comes out, shirtless and sweaty, and says, "Howdy, welcome!" His tattoos suggested he was a marine in the past. Don't worry," he says, *"my dog Tiger is all tied-up."*

We entered this poor shack of a home. Momma came out to meet us. The babies also greeted us with warm welcoming smiles. They were healthy looking, happy infant girls who were just beginning to walk. After some preliminary, getting to know us small talk, Robert finally asked, "Can I see the babies' room?"

Momma leads the way. When passing the parent's bedroom, I noticed dirty clothes stacked high on the bedroom floor. She notices that I noticed, and says, "I was just about to do the laundry."

A look in the kitchen revealed significant safety hazards: knives and sharp tools were in reach of the children; there was overflowing trash and dangerous chemicals under the sink. Many bugs were everywhere. "This place will not pass inspection," I remarked.

"Well the state people were here and did a Home Study. They said it was okay," she declared. "But I'll fix these *little* problems if you insist."

"How about your dog, did he have all his shots?" Miriam asked.

"Yes, but I'll have to find their papers next time you visit."

"What kind of dog is it?" Robert asked.

"He's a very loving Pit-Bull!" Momma replies.

I immediately searched in my pocket for my pepper spray, and took the safety lid off, just in case. "Any problems with the dog and the babies?" we asked.

"No, they get along fine," poppa says. "He's really gentle compared to the two dogs next door."

"What happened with them?" Miriam inquires.

"These two big Sheppard dogs jumped over our fence and attacked our chickens," he says.

"We ended up having fried chicken and soup all week long," Momma added.

"We'll shoot them with my shotgun, if they dare come on our lot again," her husband remarks.

Now we have three potentially serious issues: (1) a Pit-Bull dog that may not have had all required shots; (2) Dogs next door who attacked their chickens, and could be a probable danger to the babies; (3) A loaded shotgun in the house, with two children who are now beginning to walk, and are very curious. We contacted the CM later and alerted her to resolve these potential major safety problems, *ASAP*.

State budget limitations probably deters inspectors' from *fully* checking out homes, although it is likely that someone just looked the other way, since the state is pleased to get *anyone*, especially a relative willing to adopt. It saves the state lots of money and resources if relatives take responsibility for children that are in the system. We insisted that all safety issues be corrected promptly for the sake of the infants. (Our follow-up emails to the CM, with copies to her supervisor got some immediate action).

This GAL is a more direct than my spouse, who had all that excellent psychological training and P. C. awareness as an educator. When she was teaching, Miriam was *required* to be "politically correct." I am not, and never will be a PC enthusiast. Anyway, we complement each other—*most of the time*.

GAL lawyers also tell us: "Listen, we cannot expect to find 'ideal families' for these poor children. We have to accept reality; *it's as good as it gets*, under these circumstances."

While we agree with the practical reality for poor families and cases, *we cannot and will not accept* putting children in conditions that are *hazardous*, which can cause them harm by being locked into a life and environment of misery, a life without hope.

These poor, disadvantaged parents truly cared for these infant girls. They have provided for all their needs—*especially real love*.

**Lessons Learned:** Some seemingly big problems just might have reasonable solutions. Do not label people by just what you see or hear. Dig deeper below the surface. Poor disadvantaged folks can be *more loving*, than many of the richer families. If danger exists for the child, do not wait for corrective action; do whatever is possible to get quick effective results. *Raise hell with your management!* Put yourself in the shoes of parents, caregivers, the CM, especially the children. *With God's grace, all is possible.*

# SOCIOPATH CASE

This case reads like a fictional novel. Tragically, it's a true story based on actual events in the lives of the parents and their five children. It began about seven years ago, when Kemal, citizen of a middle-east country, met Lucy in 2005. Lucy had two children and a serious addiction problem. In order to remain in America, Kemal needed a green card, so they agreed to marry (which is probably immigration fraud). After about three years, Kemal abandoned Lucy, doubtless because he could not afford her cocaine habit (he was *allegedly* one of the suppliers), nor was he able to support her two children (especially another man's kids). Lucy was in and out of jails. Nevertheless, they remained "officially married" for years. (It is relatively easy to get married; but can be very difficult and much more expensive to get divorced).

Unbelievable, but true, another woman, Elisabeth (Liz), divorced her husband, years later, who *allegedly* sexually abused her and their male child. He escaped to a middle-eastern country with their boy, *forever*. She meets Kemal, and Liz then gives birth to Jonathan. The couple develops a "paramour" relationship. Kemal supplies Liz with Crack/Cocaine (according to CPI records, because "she begged him to help her"). He complains to the CPI that Liz's habit *"costs him up to $100 per day."*

The following year, Alice was born to Liz and Kemal, that was her *third addicted baby*, which required over one month of special care in the hospital (taxpayer cost is estimated at over $65,000 for each addicted infant that required extraordinary care; that's about $200,000 for three children). Months later, the parents are adjudicated "failure to protect" by the Judge X, and given a Case Plan. Kemal then says, "I'm ending my relationship with Elisabeth; the children are my priority." Nevertheless, they remain together. Kemal later complains, "I wake up and all my money is missing; I can't control this woman."

We accepted this challenging case at this stage. Our first goal was to interview the parents of the three children at their apartment in Seminole. The mother began with "her story" of how difficult it was to get off her addiction, "I'm really clean now! We plan to get married next month as soon as we get our refund of $6,000 from the IRS (all of their dependent children were actually in state foster care the prior year). They failed to inform us that daddy was still married to Lucy in another state. It's all a pack of lies, but they're not under oath, so many parents get away with deceitfulness. (Even if they are under oath, the court rarely takes any action, since it's difficult to show "intent").

The Judge, overrules GAL's objections, and allows mom custody of her latest addicted baby. "I'm really off my habit, she claims. "I'm reducing my Methadone treatment."

"These GALs recommend you *not* reduce your methadone treatment too rapidly; be sure to consult a doctor first."

Soon after our meeting, mom takes $2,000 of the *illegal* IRS refund from daddy, runs off with a known drug dealer, and buys more pills. (IRS frauds are not GAL's concern we are informed. That is a federal case, and not part of the dependency justice system).

CPI has evidence that she's again doing drugs, and again removes all the children to a foster care home, which is now approved by the same Judge X, due to "parent's failure to protect and abuse of illegal pills." They are evicted from their second apartment for failure to pay rent.

Kemal is dismissed from his third job for unknown reasons. His boss refuses to respond to GAL questions. We visit Mother once more. She has a bloody nose and black eyes. Kemal says, "It was caused by her drug deal that went bad."

The parents abruptly go-off to Alabama, abandoning their three children to the foster care provider. Kemal gets a job as a used car dealer, lives at Liz mother's home. Elizabeth one evening meets her high-school boyfriend, Tom Jones in a bar. They get married a few days later. (Is this what the Tom Jones song, *"It's not unusual to be loved by you"* means?) New husband, Mr. Jones has a long criminal record, did hard time in jail, and has children of his own from a prior marriage. Meanwhile, Liz goes to the Alabama Regional Hospital for her bladder infection. She releases herself, after getting what she really wanted, a *pain killer prescription*.

Kemal curses Liz to these GALs: "she a prostitute for drug and cigarette money," he claims. He heads back to Florida, absolutely disgusted and depressed. He calls GAL for sympathy and support. We advise him to contact his court-appointed attorney. Once again, he "bad-mouths" Elisabeth, with us: "She stole all my prescribed pills (Valium) and does 'tricks' for money in Alabama." (Liz later denies all these claims). His "Islamic doctor," believes his sad story and gives him another prescription for Valium.

Some weeks later, Elisabeth returns to Florida, moves in again with Kemal at his apartment, and now she is pregnant from her husband, Mr. Jones. Nevertheless, she is allowed by the fourth CM on the case to visit her three previously abandoned children, supervised by Caseworkers. Daughter Sally says, *"Mom, I thought you were dead?"*

Kemal claims he's father of her child (later proven false by a paternity test). He is unemployed, has insufficient income, owes $1,800 in back rent, the electric is turned off, and they are once again evicted. (Renters generally need to receive 30 days written official notice to be finally evicted).

Do we see a pattern here? Two emotionally, physically and sexually abused women become seriously addicted to cocaine and illegal pills. Two men (both happen to be from the same Islamic country), support the drug abuse habits of their "paramours." Two women give birth to multiple children. The children are neglected due to lack of parental responsibility, drug addiction, insufficient income and poor housing.

It *gets more fascinating.* Now Tallassee higher-ups and local top management get involved. The fifth CM is a seasoned trouble-shooter; he is more experienced at closing cases, and has authority to do whatever it takes to close this damn case. (His future promotion to supervisor depends on this case closing).

The Department of Children and Families (DCF) provides all kinds of referral services for the parents. Services include: in-home couples counseling, and mother's therapist services, medication management, food stamps, subsidized housing, free beds, free daycare for three of the children, among other various government services, including false teeth for mom (cocaine/crack addiction destroyed her teeth), and court appointed attorneys for each parent, all at taxpayer expense.

CM asks Mother at Staffing, "Would you like to have daycare for your infant as well?"

"Sure, if that's possible. Then I can have more time for myself."

GAL asks, "Isn't that expensive?"

"Don't worry about that," he replies, "it's covered by Head Start."

Mother then says, "I hoping to get Social Security benefits because of my bipolar condition and habitual addiction problem."

**Isn't this a great country!**

The Department of Children and Families (DCF) is determined to close this case, *no matter what!* Us GALs are getting in the way of "progress" by asking inane questions. Everyone is now against us: the State of Florida (ASA), the fifth CM and his supervisor (three of other CMs quit or were asked to resign), the parent's two defense lawyers fight us with court petitions and motions. Even the judge "signals," during the court hearing, that she favors reunification. GAL management is also ready to "throw-in the towel." We are on very thin ice. Everyone is in "Cover Your Ass" (CYA) mode. However, we are determined to fight the battle against these forces, *no matter what may come.*

As the plot thickens, a few factual errors creep into "official" court documents: The Home Study contains many errors and omissions, which are provable. Substance abuse tests were negative, but they ignored failures to show-up for other tests (considered automatic positives). Smoking was passed-over, even though three of the children have serious lung problems, verified by their doctor. Confirmed child molesters live only a few blocks away from their home. Mr. Tom Jones was not legally served; the last infant was clearly his.

At the next Staffing meeting, the CM assistant director Ms. Pompous paints a rosy picture of *disadvantaged* parents that have really "gotten their act together." (She was one of those who survived ECA's 80% turnover problem, and was promoted). GAL points out that there were "many starts, but few finishes" in the parent's case plan. The supercilious staffing leader remarks, "You appear to be biased against these parents."

My response is, "No, I'm only biased for the best interest of the children."

She then asks, "Can we have Reunification *without* GAL approval?"

The State Assistant DA responds, "The law requires a court hearing before a judge."

At the next hearing, the judge believes most of this bullshit from defense lawyers, the State, and the new CM. The judge says, "These GALs have made some very interesting and valid arguments. Nevertheless, I overrule them at this time, and approve overnights for the parents on weekends, so that better bonding can take place."

Someone once said: "If you give someone enough rope, they will hang themselves." Our strategy was exactly that! Let these parents *think* they won. Give them lots of rope; it will likely produce greater emotional stress, and that will eventually result in serious parental problems. With a bit of luck, the parents might make mistakes. (The children would be partly exposed, but they could not be insulated from this crap anyway).

## Playing by New Rules

By October, DCF in Tallassee changed the rules *substantially*. From now on GALs *must ignore all* earlier parental screw-ups, before the last JR. *No exceptions allowed!* One of the reasons for this policy, if truth be told, was too many cases were clogging the system.

These GALs were willing to play by the new rule, until others did not play by the same rules. In court hearings, they cited many "negative" UA tests, going back a year, without any discussion of missed tests during the same timeframe. They talked about parental visitations from the past, but ignored recent missed visits. Finally, they said the Home Study was approved, yet they didn't look into the serious errors.

We were convinced that at least one of the parents must be mentally ill. However, we are not psychologists. Our original GAL attorney agreed with us that the parents would probably act irrationally when stressed, after the birthing of their next baby.

Nobody expected these parents to strikeout so ferociously against us. As this case heats up, after more than two years of failure of the parents to complete their case plans, the attacks begin against us GALs, and the foster care provider. We report that we saw drug paraphernalia inside the father's vehicle. The parents then accuse us of illegally breaking into their car. (The earlier CM could not take this stress anymore and quit). Officials *must* investigate these crazy accusations against anyone. There were "no findings." The police found zero evidence to support their rash claims.

Next, a formal police complaint was made, alleging "child abuse" against the foster caregivers by the parents. Police sent the children to an unknown shelter, while the investigation continued. We had observed these foster parents with all the children, every month during two years, and had never witnessed any signs of inappropriate behavior. The child recanted, according to expert child investigators, who told GAL that the foster care *never touched her in her private region*. It was obvious to us that the parents coached this child to tell such nasty lies.

This showed how desperate the biological parents are. The mother has severe ADHD, bipolar disorder, causing major mood swings and other mental issues. She probably failed to take her meds and was stressed. Whatever her condition and motives were, it will hurt these innocent children, emotionally and psychologically. This clearly demonstrates that **we are all vulnerable to false and malicious accusations.** (No false police report complaint was filed).

Finally, the Judicial Review hearing was upon us. It seemed obvious to these GALs that the judge had made up her mind *before* the formal hearing, based on her preamble, "*We must all focus on the future—not on past events.*" As expected, the Judge decides for Reunification. We were disgusted with her verdict. But we would not "rubber stamp" other people's *misguided decisions*.

**Our Closing Statement:** Your honor, we *strongly object* to reunification at this time, because these parents have *not* changed their behaviors since the last JR. We cannot expect addicted parents to change completely in a mere few months. *That is unrealistic!* These parents, and their children, have certainly been through lots of stress. However, the source of this stress was the result of *their appalling behavior*. They will certainly experience even greater stresses when reunited with five very young, active children. They have had many state provided referrals. Now they must take responsibility for their own family. These Guardians were voices for the **Best Interest of the Children.**

After the JR hearing, we thought about the judge's opening statement. How can anyone determine the future, *without* considering recent history? If one connects the dots on sordid behaviors, one can predict the outcome. (Ironically, about six months later, we learned that the father had an accident and he was prescribed Oxycodone for many months. The result was he became addicted). *What goes around comes around!*

**Lessons Learned:** One has to choose their battles. Once one loses creditability with ECA, CM, and ADA, it becomes very difficult to fight for the children. Sometimes we have to "suck-up" to managers, even when it's distasteful to get positive results for the children. Winning is not always possible, but one has to fight the "good battle," and leave an "official record" for DCF and future court hearings. Why didn't these GALs report the father's Green Card fraud to Immigration authorities. First, if the father was deported, he might take the children with him to an Islamic country; that might result in the children going from the "frying pan into the fire." Second, if the dad left the mother alone with her children, she would most not be able to cope financially and emotionally. Third, vengeance is not the Christian way—we leave the Lord to deal with retribution.

# DISADVANTAGED CASE

This is the case of a disadvantaged child, born into a very poor family, in Puerto Rico. Her father died from an accident, a month before her birth. The underprivileged mother of the children had no accident insurance or Social Security back then. She had to care not only for this precious child, but also for three older sisters, and afterward, the aged grandfather and grandmother came to live with them, on one salary. The mother's job was cooking for a Catholic school in the village on the island.

It was the post-war years of the mid-1940s. A big pot of chicken soup with lots of veggies was the typical main meal, most of the week. The early years for this little girl were difficult, yet joyful. Her mother had to be very strict with all four girls, but *lovingly so*. She taught them the fundamental teachings of the Christian faith and basic morality at home; and she actually lived by that belief and trust in Jesus Christ, every day.

As the child reached the age of seven, her mother saw that she was interested in teaching. Many of the local children would gather around her after school, when she would play at teaching with them and her little blackboard. It was time for a major decision by the Mother. This decision would change this child's life forever. Because the Mother loved her daughter so much, she decided to send her to New York City to live with her Aunt. She believed that the life and education system would be much better there. That was an *extremely difficult and emotional* decision for the mother, and especially for the little seven-year old child.

The child moved to New York City, in an ethnic minority community, with her two cousins, sharing one bedroom. The Aunt was a very kind and *loving caregiver*, although her husband was *dysfunctional*, and *an absolute tyrant*. Her other Aunt looked after her as well, and acted like a "second mother," during her early teen years and beyond. She went to a school in downtown New York. It was an excellent school and she had many good *role models* as classmates. Later, the teenager had to study hard, but did well in this challenging, highly academic high school, and went on to college.

Now as a young adult, she had to have strong character and *spirit* to be able to work days, and attend college classes at night. She frequently did not have enough money to buy dinner, and would arrive back at the Aunt's apartment at 10 PM, hungry and exhausted. Nevertheless, she saved her hard-earned money to pay for college expenses. After this long four-year struggle, she finally earned a BA in Education. (Years later, she worked days and took night courses, and earned her Master's in Special Education).

Immediately after college, she met a handsome young man from a *very different culture* and environment, and they fell in love. However, they both believed in those "old Christian traditions"; they did not have sex until *after* they were married, eighteen months later. Her teaching job kept her busy. They worked and saved, and struggled to make ends meet and to pay the typical bills of apartment living in the big city. No one gave them a "free ride." They were poor and struggled to survive, but *rich in Christian Spirit*.

When she became pregnant, her first duty was to be a real mother, *a true parent*. Her first priority was to *nurture and love* this little girl, that special gift from God, and the two additional gifts He gave them, a few years later. She was a devoted Christian, dedicated and passionate teacher, and she spent many hours at night teaching all three children *ethical behavior*, and the essentials of Christ's teachings. Dad was busy earning a living to support this family of five, and trying to climb higher on the corporate ladder so that someday they might buy a home and settle in a nice suburban community.

Not all was perfect in their life, *it never is*. Grief comes with that package called life. Have you ever known anyone who *never* experienced grief in life? Her mother and aunt all died during the same week, suddenly in 1980. Months later her sister died. Other difficulties occurred that were troubling during those many years of marriage.

Meanwhile, both parents focused on the importance of an early good education, and *insisted* that all three children go to college (and earn part of the cost themselves with summer jobs). Today, they all have college degrees, earn excellent wages in the corporate world of business, and are self-sufficient. She cried when she learned her students, in the 2005 Yearbook, elected her "Best Teacher."

**Lessons learned by Miriam:**
What are some of the lessons from this simple, yet perhaps not so common story? (This child, who became a wonderful mother, a grandmother, and an *extraordinary* teacher, is Miriam, my fantastic wife, and fellow Guardian). In my view some lessons learned from Miriam's "disadvantaged" case and her long journey in life on planet Earth are:

1. Love is doing what is *good* for the one you love, even if it sometimes hurts. In this case, it was giving up a precious child to someone else, for Miriam's benefit. Her mother was unselfish in this very difficult decision to do what is best for her daughter. Miriam was never resentful or angry. She never blamed her mother for this difficult, self-sacrificing decision. *That is what real love is all about!*

2. Miriam took *responsibility* for all of her own acts in life. The way to learn this key lesson is to insist that children share in the family chores and contribute to the welfare of the *family* as a whole. For example, let them earn part of the cost of college and other obligations in life they will encounter. There is "no free ride in life." Adversity and challenges builds character. There is no "free ride." If one is sheltered from all failure, they will certainly not experience true success.
3. Good role models and peer-groups are critical. Do not allow your kids to hang out with bizarre immoral characters. Mothers and fathers must take responsibility for whomever influences your children, and must control that "window into the world," the TV and Internet.
4. Miriam's Aunt, was her "guardian angel" (and still is today at age 97), who looked out for her welfare. Miriam was protected in a tough neighborhood, which was very poor and challenging for any family to bring up a child.
5. Faith in God was *essential* for her to overcome years of trying moments growing up in a big city environment, in times of crisis, of which there were many.

> *Only a life lived for others is a life worthwhile.*
> —Albert Einstein

Nationally, cases of child abuse and neglect have fallen sharply since the early '90s, according a federal government study. *'Only'* 553,000 children suffered physical, emotional, or sexual abuse in 2005-6, the study found, down 26% from 743,200 abuse victims in 1993. We think that over half a million-reported cases is *unacceptable.*

During 2001-2010, about 30.8 million child abuse and neglect cases (cumulatively) were reported nationally. In 2011-2012, cost for non-fatal short/long-term health care was $25B, child welfare services was $4.5B, criminal justice was $3.9B, special education was $4.3B, and the estimated productivity losses were $83.6B, for a total of $121.6 billion annually. Consequently, Congress passed H.R. 6655 (the Protect Our Kids Act of 2012), to establish a commission to Eliminate Child Abuse and Neglect Fatalities.

According to Florida's DCF, abused and neglected children in 2011-2012, totaled about 53,000 children; and 83% were under the age of five. During that same period, Healthy Families served 8,475 high-risk families and their 15,066 children.

Nationally, perpetrators of *all confirmed* child abuse or neglect cases in 2010, by caregiver are the mother alone (26.4%), mom and dad together (22%), and non-parents (13.4%). A typical profile was a young adult (in their mid-20s), without high school diploma, below the poverty level, very depressed, who had difficulty coping with stressful situations. About 78% of all children's cases did not receive proper food, clothing, shelter, hygiene, education, medical care or protection.

The population of our *sample states* are California (38m), Texas (26m), NY (20m), Florida (20m), and Illinois (13m). Interestingly, the Department of Children and Families (DCF) budget in 2012 of Florida was $2.8 billion, while California was only $1.8 billion.

While statistics are interesting, we are dealing with innocent, precious, real human beings. We have only provided a small sample of *real cases* and the "human challenges" faced in New York, Colorado, Illinois, Arizona, and California, which follows:

## New York Cases

In 2009, New York State had 164,831 cases, compared with 161,580 cases in 2008. Three of the larger, wealthier NY counties have had a greater number of cases in 2009: Nassau (6,688), Suffolk (10,053), and Westchester (6,127).

This Bronx NYC case came in from a "concerned citizen," alleging that there was domestic violence between the biological mother and her boyfriend (not his children). When I spoke to the source of the report (which is a required protocol in NYC), it was not long before the source accidentally revealed that she was the mother of this boyfriend. She then begged me not to tell her son that she called in the report. "I am not permitted to disclose the source, unless it is revealed during court trial," I assured her. Clearly, I knew this woman must be concerned since she called in a report against her own son.

Under NYC mandate, we must make a face-to-face contact with ALL children (or try our damned best) within 24 hours of receiving the report. That night I went to the home unannounced. The boyfriend answered the door. He was a 30-year old Hispanic, Jose, who was soon "sweating bullets." Mom was not home. In fact, the boyfriend was watching her two baby boys while mom was at the "pain management specialist" (this will tie-in later). Jose put mom on the phone who said she won't be back for a while, and asked if I would come back the following day? I was required to do an assessment of the home and children's situation to determine if they were safe (at least for that night).

The surprising thing was that Jose was doing a good job of babysitting, despite the fact that he was as nervous as a "virgin at a prom. He was trying to put the boys, aged five and six to bed. They were jumping up and down on their beds and otherwise fooling around. The boyfriend asked me not to interview the boys as the mother directed him to have me wait until I met her. I could see that the children didn't have any marks or bruises; they were adequately clothed and had more than up-to-par sleeping arrangements. There was more than adequate food in the home, and piles of toys, and the home was clean. I was sure the children would survive that night.

The next day I met mom in the afternoon. The kids were in school and Jose was no longer there. Mom was ready; the place was spotless. I sat with her at the kitchen table. She was a Hispanic woman, in her late thirties. She assured me that her two young boys were better cared for than any other children on this earth were. I couldn't help noticing her slurred speech while her eyes rolled back, and then they focused on me. When I asked mom if she was on any meds, she listed more than ten, including oxycodone and zanex. This seemed normal to her as she listed a dozen health problems.

Mom then asked me how old I was and if I was single. I told her this was too personal. She then raised the bar and said, "I will kick my boyfriend out of the house. "On your next visit, please call me in advance. I'll make you dinner, honey." I changed the subject and asked her to go to a nearby center and have a urine test. Mom declined, but showed me some of her prescriptions and the doctor's phone number. This turned out to be useless since the doc refused to return my calls.

I left the home that day sure that not only was she abusing drugs, but there was something fishy involving the boyfriend Jose, as well. Under NYC mandate, I cannot interfere with parental rights unless I can prove the children are in imminent danger. Upon further investigation, I learned that both boys had missed a substantial amount of school.

What was most helpful was the phone number of the paternal grandmother, given to me by the source of the original report (Jose's mother). Grandma was living out of state, but close to my own mom's home. Grandma was concerned for her grandchildren, and she not only made it a point that she was not happy with her daughter's boyfriend; she wanted custody of her grandchildren, if we had to remove them from mom's care. (I said nothing that even hinted of the possibility of removal). So clearly, something was going on here and everyone seemed to be in on it but me.

Another week went by, during which time mom again declined urine tests and refused to come to my office for a Family Team Conference (FTC). The boyfriend, Jose, was M.I.A., and legally "my hands were tied." I visited the boys and learned that the oldest child might be held back in school due to excessive absences.

Then I made a milestone as I did what every CPS (sort of CPI and CM mix) should do (or at least attempt to do) in this situation; I contacted the biological father. Dad "spilled the beans" and told me that not only is mom on illegal drugs, but the boyfriend is selling them to her and many others. Why didn't he call in a report sooner? Still we had no case without dirty urine or an arrest, and mom was avoiding us like the plague. Jose vanished off the face of the planet by this time.

The weekend came and went. I came in early on the following Monday. My supervisor looked at me and said, "Is this your case? You've got a problem." All he knew was that the boys were at the hospital, with possible oxycodone in their system. When I got to the hospital, the police informed me that over the weekend, mom made the children peanut and jelly sandwiches. The boys did not like that type of jelly and they gave it to the neighbor's child, who was about one year younger. When the neighbor's mother examined the sandwich to see if it contained any peanut butter (her child was allergic), she discovered the real secret ingredients: four oxycodone pills. The irate neighbor called the police, and subsequently mom attempted suicide on the spot, by swallowing dozens of pills—a cocktail mixture of everything she had.

We may never know how the oxycodone got into the sandwiches. When I asked the oldest child, he said, "They must have fallen off the kitchen shelf." My guess is that mommy left her pills out on the table and the children found them, and decided to play "Betty Crocker" with mom's painkillers. Anyway, mom should never have been "high" while watching her kids and these meds should have been secured out of reach of her young children.

**Lessons Learned:** This story had a blessing in disguise and a happy conclusion. It turned out that no children were harmed. We had more than we needed to remove the kids; and mom did not die although she was admitted into the hospital psychiatric unit. Dad came forward to claim his kids. We required him to do a basic case plan, including parenting skill classes and UA's, since he should have known that his children were in danger. The judge sent the boys home the following week. Mom faced criminal charges for endangering the safety and welfare of her kids. Mom's "Pain Management Specialist" finally returned my messages. After further investigation, the "pain killer" doctor underwent trial, did some time in jail and lost his license. In summary, a potential chaos turned into a positive conclusion for the mom, the father and his children, and it turned out to be one more "pill mill" closed down.

## NYC Family Service Unit Investigator Interview

1. **How different is NYC Child Protection/Support system vs. Florida?**
   CPI in Florida is CPS (Child Protective Specialist) in NYC.
   NYC has a much greater population of diverse cultures.

2. **Key issues & challenges in NYC?**
   Administration for Children Services (ACS) in NYC has a "horrible" reputation in the media. The court, the schools, and medical staff consider them "incompetent." Layoffs have been high recently, which adds more cases to the limited staff.

3. **Number of cases per supervisor (similar to CM) in Family Service Unit (FSU)?**
   About 15-20 cases; of these perhaps 12 cases need visits and supervision. We have about 4-5 cases per week (average) under Protective Diagnostic (PD), that require court action.

4. **What are the major problems/challenges?**
   Layoffs: Less workers means more work for under Protective Diagnostic (PD), Family Service Unit (FSU), and other paid specialists. Morale: We don't like being labeled "incompetent" by

New Yorkers. Fear: Everyone is alarmed about media reports of child deaths and turnover rates.

5. **How would you make it better?**
   Improve public relations. Motivate and keep more workers. Lower case loads and lower turnover rates. We need many more CASA or Guardian ad Litem participation.

6. **What are the types of crime by reported cases?**
   Drugs, domestic violence, sex abuse are the key problems. For example, in Staten Island prescription drug abuse is an epidemic. Brooklyn has too many child fatalities. All boroughs have cocaine problems.

## Colorado Cases

Child advocates push for more openness in abuse, neglect cases. By Jennifer Brown *the Denver Post* (Condensed for this book).

When four boys who could not speak or use the bathroom were rescued from a filthy Denver apartment, seven years after three older siblings were taken from the same parents, child protection authorities had this to say: *Nothing.* They believed they were bound by confidentiality law from saying anything about the case, even as public outrage grew and blame was heaped on Denver County child welfare.

Human services authorities will not say whether they received any calls to the child abuse hotline, as the family's neighbors said they made [many calls]. Nor whether they visited the home in the years since the first three kids [reported issues]. Not even whether they went to court to ask a judge to remove the boys born after their parents lost a court battle to keep their first three children. Instead, the community was left in the dark.

Across the nation, child advocates are pushing for more transparency in child abuse and neglect cases, arguing that *confidentiality impedes reform* and that it is possible to answer questions about how the system broke down without violating a child's privacy.

"Confidentiality is killing kids," said Michael Petit, president of *Every Child Matters* in Washington, D.C. *"It's shielding the public from what the real problems are. It isn't just the public's right to know, it's the public's right to intervene."*

Colorado rewrote part of its transparency law this year, requiring that a state review team that investigates child deaths include age, gender and a description of any previous involvement with child welfare authorities. The reviews also identify problems for the county that handled the case. By the time the reports are released, sometimes a year after the death and after a back-and-forth process of state and county input, public outcry has quieted. In addition, the public and the media do not have access to the original documents.

Colorado's child ombudsman, a watchdog for the state's child welfare system, found earlier this year that the Child Fatality Review Team made 97 errors of fact and missing details when reviewing the death of a 2-year-old boy whose skeleton was found under his home. The state did not include all policy mistakes made by caseworkers who had received calls about the boy before his meth-using mother strangled him, the ombudsman said.

So far, 40 children in Colorado died from abuse and neglect, according to a state website required to list the incidents within three days. About one quarter of those children's families were involved with child welfare workers within 3-years of their deaths.

The tally of kids who were killed, nearly killed—including severe brain injuries—and egregiously neglected—including the four Denver boys rescued from squalor in September—is at 85 for this year. Of those, 33 were previously known to the child protective system, meaning a state team is required to review those cases.

This year's law change also requires that Colorado's fatality reviews include the names of children who have been killed, but not those still living. The state Department of Human Services previously released the names of children killed by abuse and neglect, but made the reports nameless when the state began putting them online. State officials said they changed policy to align with federal guidelines.

The Denver Post used state fatality reviews that included children's names to create an online gallery of children's stories and photos. The newspaper's investigation last year found that 40 percent of children who die of abuse and neglect in this state had families who were previously known to caseworkers. ...

Reform advocates are not arguing that laws to protect privacy are not necessary. Revealing the name of a girl sexually assaulted by her uncle, for example, serves no purpose, reform advocates say. However, the public should know how the child protection system works, or doesn't, so people can participate politically in reform.

**"Children, in particular dead children, do not have a voice,"** she said. "When we hide that horribleness from all of the good people, there is nobody good standing up and saying we need more help and we need more resources. Instead, we are talking about resources for those who have a voice."

**Where were the Guardian ad Litem volunteers? Independent oversight and investigation by experienced GALs might have saved these children.**

Enoch A. Hayslett brought his 1-month-old son to a hospital emergency room in December 2008, saying the baby was constipated. Instead, doctors found the infant had a broken femur—an injury Hayslett and the child's mother couldn't explain. Therefore, the Illinois Department of Children and Family Services took protective custody of the baby and his two older siblings, and a Cook County judge ordered that all three children be placed in foster care.

Hayslett and their mother went on to have more children: a daughter, another son, then twin boys—all of whom lived with the couple in the south suburbs as they sought to regain custody of the three older children. During that time, DCFS twice investigated complaints that Hayslett was abusing his children but found the allegations not credible, records show.

Then—a month after a child-protection investigator closed the second case—the 5-foot-10, 280-pound Hayslett was charged with beating one of his twin sons to death. The 20-pound boy's skull was fractured, and he had multiple bruises. They arrested the Lynwood man in December 2012 and charged him with first-degree murder, among other charges. Last Father's Day, Hayslett hanged himself at the Cook County Jail.

His 8-month-old son Lamar Hayslett was among 27 Illinois children to die from abuse or neglect in DCFS' last reporting year after they or their families already had been involved with the agency, a Chicago Sun-Times and WBEZ examination of newly released records from the DCFS inspector general's office has found. Five more cases were under investigation, those records show.

On Wednesday, the head of child-death investigations for DCFS Inspector General Denise Kane said that one of those five pending cases has now been determined not to have involved abuse or neglect. A second case remains under investigation, but not for abuse or neglect. Still, the number of DCFS-involved abuse or neglect deaths could reach 30 for the third year in a row.

In the 2010 reporting year, there were 15 abuse or neglect deaths in which DCFS had had some involvement with the family within a year of the death, according to a Sun-Times and WBEZ investigation published in November. The spike in deaths to 34 in 2011, 34 in 2012 and 27 or more in 2013 has sounded alarms with state lawmakers and some child advocates, who say the agency and the private contractors it hires to monitor child safety are not doing the job they should. ...

Still, in response to the Sun-Times/WBEZ reports, DCFS' acting director, Denise Gonzales, ordered a review of all child deaths resulting from abuse or neglect between 2009 and 2013. That review revealed errors in the departments tracking of how many children statewide died from abuse or neglect, finding that 11 more children had died in that time than the agency had reported.

Of the 27 DCFS-involved abuse or neglect deaths reported for the 12 months ending June 30, 2013, 12 were caused by abuse and 15 caused by neglect, according to the Sun-Times/WBEZ examination of DCFS inspector general records. Of the neglect deaths, 11 involved infants smothered or suffocated after being placed in dangerous sleeping conditions.

In many of those cases, the children died even though their caregivers had been trained on safe-sleep practices, records show. They included a 3-month-old girl who died after sleeping on a mattress with her father, who "tested positive for cocaine, marijuana and prescribed benzodiazepines," according to the inspector general's case summary. A caseworker had provided the mother with a Pack 'n Play portable crib and saw the baby with the mother in August and October 2012. The baby died the following month.

**Among the 12 child abuse deaths.**

A 14-year-old autistic boy, Alex Spourdalakis, of River Grove, was found stabbed to death in his bed in June 2013. His 50-year-old mother and 44-year-old live-in caretaker lay unconscious next to him, "having taken pills" and "leaving a letter explaining their actions." DCFS had opened a neglect investigation into his mother six months earlier but found the allegations not credible. The mother and caretaker survived and are now charged with murder.

A 5-month-old girl, Angelina Rodriguez, of Chicago's Far North Side, died in April 2013, four days after being hospitalized with a skull fracture and severe brain swelling. Her parents both were charged with murder after her father admitted suffocating her. Three months before Angelina died, school officials called DCFS' hotline to report her 6-year-old brother had "marks and bruises on his face, neck and arms and after getting sick, he expressed fear of going home early." DCFS cleared the parents of wrongdoing because the child later told an investigator the marks were made by his 2-year-old brother.

In a case of the death of a child whose teenage mother had been an abuse victim, 3-week-old Emonie Beasley-Brown was killed in August 2012 when her mother ran away from her South Side home, taking the baby to her boyfriend's house. When the police showed up, the mother hid in a crawlspace with the baby and her boyfriend's mother, who placed her hands over Emonie's mouth to keep her from crying. Emonie died two days later as a result of suffocation. Emonie's teenage mother was convicted of endangering the life and health of a child and sentenced to five years of probation. Her boyfriend's mother was convicted of the same charge and sentenced to four years in prison. In January 2012, DCFS had determined that Emonie's mother had been abused earlier that month by her 17-year-old brother, who was a ward of the state.

DCFS officials point out that they are involved with about 60,000 families a year. Child-welfare experts caution the agency shouldn't be judged solely on the fraction of children who die while they or their families are being monitored or under investigation by the agency. Still, acting DCFS chief Gonzales says she's convened "a team to read every case and tell me what happened. . . . What were the conditions that brought us to that child's death? Was there substance abuse involved?

Was there domestic violence involved? Was this just a tired mom with her infant?"

In the case of Lamar Hayslett, Cook County Public Guardian Robert Harris says there were "missed opportunities" to stop the abuse. Besides the two abuse investigations against Enoch Hayslett that DCFS closed without finding wrongdoing, a Cook County judge was told in August 2011 of allegations that Hayslett had abused the three older children in foster care. The judge left it to a private agency, Lutheran Social Services, to determine whether the parents should continue to have unsupervised visits with those kids. Those visits were temporarily suspended and then resumed, leading to more allegations from one of Hayslett's children that he was abusing them—complaints DCFS deemed not credible the month before Lamar died. ...

Says Harris: "The fact that there was a hotline call that was made just three months before Lamar died, in and of itself, which subsequently was 'unfounded' a month before he died is definitely troubling to me, and I question some of the investigator's work in terms of responding to the hotline call.

"I don't just want to say 'If the caseworkers were doing their jobs.' But if they had kept their eyes open to all of these multiple factors, maybe there could have been—maybe Lamar wouldn't have had to have died."

**Did they appoint Guardians (GAL or CASA) to these cases? If not, why not?**

**Times/WBEZ reader's response:** If you were to read similar annual DCFS reports from past years, they would be remarkably similar. That is the problem. These children, and their families, had prior contact with DCFS, which is funded by taxpayers at about $1.5 billion a year. DCFS, like all Illinois state agencies, is a political pork farm, especially under the Democrats over the last 11 years. Nevertheless, there is plenty of money left over to reduce the number of preventable fatalities. What is needed is leadership and innovation, which appears to be lacking in an election year. If DCFS' current leadership is not up to the job, they should check out what other states are doing. No doubt there is high-quality research going on somewhere in the country, both at the academic and practical level, and DCFS should find it and emulate it, since there is virtually no innovation here in Illinois, despite the enormous resources we taxpayers provide.

**Note: See the Appendix for more details on many Illinois cases.**

## Arizona Cases

About 6,000 cases of suspected child abuse or neglect that were reported to a statewide Arizona hotline over the past four years were *never investigated*, officials disclosed Thursday, calling it reason for "grave alarm."

A team at Arizona's Child Protective Services agency improperly designated the cases "N.I."—meaning "Not Investigated"—to help manage the heavy workload and focus on the most severe cases, said Clarence Carter, chief of the state's child welfare system.

Under state law, all reports generated via the hotline must be investigated, Carter said. All the cases will be reviewed, officials said. At least 125 cases already have been identified in which children were later alleged to have been abused, they said.

"I don't know of any fatalities," Gregory McKay, the agency's chief of child welfare investigations, said of the botched cases. No one has been disciplined, but Arizona's Department of Public Safety will investigate. "There must be accountability in this matter, and I will insist on further reforms to make sure that it cannot happen again," Gov. Jan Brewer said.

The practice of misclassifying the cases and essentially closing them started in 2009, Carter said. The number rapidly escalated in the past

20 months as caseloads increased and other changes were made, and 5,000 of the 6,000 cases happened in that time, he said.

"The idea that there are 6,000 cases where we don't know whether or not children are safe, that's cause for grave alarm," said Carter, who as director of Arizona's Department of Economic Security oversees CPS and other social welfare agencies.

CPS has been one of the governor's major priorities and has suffered from understaffing and major increases in abuse reports and workloads in recent years. Brewer got approval from the Legislature in January for emergency funding for 50 new caseworkers and regular funding for 150 more in the budget year that began July 1.

In a statement, the governor called the mishandling of the cases "absolutely unacceptable."

## California Cases

In 2012, there were 487,016 reported *allegations* of child abuse and neglect in California. Of those cases, 17% were substantiated (verified) by the state child welfare system. More than 60% of those verified cases were due to general neglect.

California's rate of substantiated cases of child abuse or neglect declined from 12.0 cases per 1,000 children ages 0-17 in 1998, to 8.9 per 1,000 children in 2012.

Neglect consistently has been the most common type of substantiated cases statewide and in nearly all counties for which these data are available. Children ages 0-5 make up the largest percentage of substantiated cases of child abuse or neglect in California; they comprised 46% of all cases in 2012, up from 40% in 1998.

Children who are abused or neglected including those who witness domestic violence, often exhibit emotional, cognitive, and behavioral problems, such as anxiety, depression, suicidal behavior, and difficulty in school, use of alcohol and other drugs, and early sexual activity.

Statewide, child abuse and neglect cases disproportionately involve children of color, particularly African American/Black and American Indian/Alaska Native children.

**How many GALs or CASA volunteers were assigned to these serious cases?**

Files detail deaths of 14 children. The abuse cases came from families that had been under scrutiny by L.A. County child welfare officials. Garrett Therolf and Kim Christensen Los Angeles Times Staff Writer

Fourteen children died of abuse and neglect in Los Angeles County last year despite coming from families that had been under the scrutiny of child welfare officials, records released Monday show.

The family of a boy who died of multiple skull fractures had been reported 25 times to the Department of Children and Family Services and the mother had a known history of methamphetamine use. In other families, children died within months or even one day after a social worker's last visit.

The records, which included previously confidential family services and police reports, medical charts and other documents, were obtained by *The Times* through a California Public Records Act request and provide the first comprehensive snapshot of child fatalities countywide.

A new state law that took effect last year loosened the confidentiality requirements that had kept most such information from public view. All told, the records show, 32 children in the county died in 2008 from abuse and neglect, including physical assault, drowning and malnourishment. Eighteen of the children were in families that had never been in contact with the family services agency.

But the other 14 families should have been well-known to child welfare officials, based on previous referrals and investigations. For whatever reasons, many of the earlier allegations were not substantiated. In 10 of those cases, the agency has launched investigations that will probably result in discipline against social workers, agency officials said.

"These are shocking cases," said county Supervisor Gloria Molina, who contends that disciplinary and training procedures need to be dramatically improved in the department. "**The biggest problem is that no lessons are learned.**"

Agency officials say they lack adequate resources to handle daunting caseloads.

The heavily redacted files paint a horrific picture of the circumstances in which the children died. Among the cases:

* A 1-year-old girl who was left alone with her mother last March, despite a court order requiring monitored visits. The girl had fallen down the stairs and hit her head, her mother told authorities, explaining that she gave the girl an ice pack, put her to bed and went back to doing the laundry.

Only three hours later, when the child's grandmother returned, did the family realize that she was unconscious. Doctors found the scenario described by the mother as "highly unlikely," concluding the girl had died of blunt force trauma "consistent with being thrown or slammed against a hard surface."

Child welfare records show the mother had history of neglect.

* Another 1-year-old girl who died May 8 after a babysitter allegedly punished her for jumping on the bed. The sitter allegedly knocked the

girl's feet out from under her and slammed her head against a dresser, according to police. Family Services had received 11 complaints to the child abuse hotline related to the baby's family. One call occurred four months before the child's death, when her 18-year-old mother was arrested for petty theft.

Police at the time discovered extensive "unexplained injuries" on the infant, including "dirty and pink eyes" and rashes on her buttocks that were "almost bleeding." Still, social workers determined that the allegation of general neglect was "inconclusive." The child remained with her mother after a social worker overruled a computer-generated recommendation that stronger action be taken.

* An 18-month-old boy who was found breathing but unconscious last May. His mother's boyfriend told them that the child had choked on a penny. When patting the boy's back didn't dislodge it, the man told medics and a sheriff's deputy, he tried to perform the Heimlich maneuver on him.

At the hospital, however, tests revealed that the boy had suffered hemorrhaging on the right side of his brain, an injury that was "indicative of shaken baby syndrome," records show. He was declared brain-dead two days later. Caseworkers had previously substantiated allegations of emotional abuse and "caretaker absence."

# HARD & SOFT JUDGES

Dependency judges vary *in the extreme*. Some judges are absolute tyrants who intimidate and scare witnesses and attorneys, such as Judge X: "CPI shut up and sit down! If I want to hear from you, I'll ask your viewpoint." "Attorney Jane, I read the TPR report; do you really have anything else to add or subtract? If not, let's move on."

This GAL prefers "no nonsense" judges. At least Judge X did not put up with lots of crap that parents and their defense attorneys try to pull in court. The real problem with Judge X was that he took 6-8 months to write his judgment, *after* his TPR decision. That delayed the appeal process, which delayed the adoption process. It was clearly not fair to all parties, especially the children, waiting for the long adoption process to begin.

At the other end of this judicial spectrum, we found that most judges are *too soft*, or pro-parents: "I want to be sure to dot all my 'I's' and cross all the 'T's,'" Judge Y said. (She was concerned that the appeal court might overturn her decisions). She also generally asked, "Can't you (State, CM, GAL, and parent's defense attorneys) resolve these issues before you come before me?" Another typical remark: I think these parents should be given another opportunity to reunite with their children. I do not see any safety issues here. In fact, this was the parent's third chance, and the children were in *imminent danger*. (Why must children be damaged before corrective action is taken?)

Finally, we experienced the firm and assertive, but "totally unrealistic" Judge Z, who demanded CM take *immediate* action and provide certain referrals and other services, and report to me within 30 days. Unfortunately, the State and CM could not realistically get approval and funding for any of these services "demanded" by this judge.

Fortunately, many judges we dealt with were mostly fair, balanced, insightful and considerate of the plight of the children." Consider this hearing from Miami-Dade:

DCF-gets-a-Grilling-from-Judges
Source: Carol Marbin Miller (Condensed for this book)

## Florida

Miami-Dade County's entire child welfare bench presided over a virtually unprecedented hearing in which the five judges grilled lawyers and an investigator with the Department of Children & Families over *"systemic"* failures that have left children dead or gravely injured.

They used the plight of a 4-year-old boy to pull back the curtain on problems occurring throughout the state. ... He has been subjected to a *"violent, unstable and dangerous home"* with the agency repeatedly refusing to remove him for his own safety. His parents have engaged in fistfights, stalking, a knifing and a kidnapping, the judge said.

The boy's father has ignored court orders to stay away from the child's mom, who has a bad drinking problem. DCF's abuse hotline has received at least three calls that domestic violence left the boy in peril *[he was clearly in imminent danger]*.

Through it all, DCF has taken no action to place him in a safer environment. The judges wanted to know why. "This is what's troubling me," said Circuit Judge Michael A. Hanzman. "The minute I read the [court records], there was no question that this was not a case where the child could be left at home. Reasonable minds could not differ. *This is what I call a no-brainer.*"

The little boy first came to the agency's attention in 2009, when the hotline received a report that his parents had been fighting violently over what DCF investigator Jose Antonio Garza described as "infidelity issues." Police arrested the father for breaking into the mother's home, locking her in a laundry room and kidnapping the child.

The investigation went nowhere, because the boy's mother told investigators she had moved to Pennsylvania—a claim [DCF] Garza later admitted might have been a lie. What is worse, the judge said, DCF apparently made no effort to determine where the then-infant was living. The case was closed, and the investigator moved on. ....

Child protection investigators got another chance to help the boy, when the hotline received a report that his mother had knifed the father. The mom—whose mental illnesses had led to at least one involuntary commitment—was arrested, and DCF "verified" the allegation that the parents' family violence was a threat to the boy's safety. Still no removal. DCF's solution this time: referring the family to a domestic violence program in Homestead. However, nobody at the agency followed up to ensure that the parents were actively "engaged" in the counseling and treatment that the program, Project SOS, had to offer. *They were not.*

... "What good are these services," asked Circuit Judge Cindy Lederman, "if the parents don't succeed in them, don't complete the program and don't modify their behavior? Isn't it dangerous to just walk away after making a referral?"

When the boy's predicament was raised yet again with DCF's child abuse hotline in 2013, DCF asked Judge Rosa Figarola to order the parents to accept the help they had rejected three years earlier. [Judge] Figarola had another idea: She ordered DCF to remove the youngster from his parents, arguing no amount of counseling could render the boy safe.

At the hearing, Judge Hanzman challenged the agency to "give me an argument or a rationale for looking at this set of facts where you leave a 4-year-old home in the circumstances of this case?"

DCF's lawyer, *refused to answer*, calling that information the agency's "work product."

[Judge] Figarola, who has presided over domestic violence cases in the past, and other judges took issue with the department's policy of claiming children are safe from spousal violence because one partner has obtained a stay-away order from the other, or because the department [DCF] has imposed a "safety plan" in which one or both parents promise to avoid violence. "Oh, we've got an injunction—now the kids are safe," Figarola said. "*Oh, my God!* If he wants to get her, he's going to get her."

During our five years as GALs, we encountered some of these judicial extremes. Nevertheless, most of the judges respect *Guardian ad Litem* volunteers, since we are the advocates for the children. In court, we are the "eyes and ears of the judge," whereas everyone else has an obvious bias. The parent's attorneys, by definition, focus on parent's rights. ADA's focus is legal issues. CMs concern is about case plan checklists. In reality, it is not just about parental rights, laws, and case plans. *It is about victim's rights*—the voiceless children, who become stuck in the dependency system.

**Where were the Guardian's *voices for the children* in these cases?**

# FOSTER CARE

*"Man is dependent on God; he is not dependent on a state. But once dependent on God is lost, then the state takes over the attributes of Divinity, and being material in its structure, crushes the last vestige of the human spirit."*
—Fulton J. Sheen

Family preservation is supposed to be the primary feature of "modern" social services. Foster care and protective services caseworkers are supposed to use their *best efforts* to reunite families. In many cases foster care has become a temporarily place to house children. This "temporary" goal has too often turned from a few months into years. Florida law requires children not to be in foster care for more than one year. *"It's the law!"* Yet, many of our cases involved kids in foster care for two years or more.

Source: *I Speak for This Child* by Gay Courter (Edited and condensed for this book).

Foster care is a growth industry! The foster care population increased from 269,000 in the mid-1980s to 460,000 in 1992, [rising to over 560,000 today]. At the same time, the number of children freed for adoption has stayed constant in the 30,000 to 40,000 range. About

100,000 additional children have adoption as their long-term plan, but most of these children never find permanent homes.

Is it true that nobody will take these hard-to-place children? In the 1960s, the point of adoption was to provide babies to infertile families based on matching characteristics including appearance, religion, and background. These days, when there are far more people who want to adopt than children, the affinity is based on tolerance. What behaviors might parents abide? Might they accept a hyperactive child? A child with a learning disability? A child of a different race? A child with a physical handicap? Would they take sexually abused children? A child who has committed a crime?

If you get a group of adoption advocates together, they soon get into a game of one-upmanship describing their least adoptable case. One distressing statistic is that the younger the age of a child entering the foster care system, the longer he stays a foster child. Fifty-three percent of the children who come into foster care remain *without* a permanent home for over four years. Doesn't it seem more likely that the cute infants would be the most adoptable? It would, except most are not available for adoption.

Family preservation is the hallmark of the "modern" social services approach. Foster care and protective services caseworkers are supposed to use their best efforts to reunite families."

## Our Foster Care Experience

There are many good foster care homes, including special medical foster care, and teenage foster care. The state inspects them for safety, hygiene and good childcare practices yearly, before reapproving their licenses. Nonetheless, Guardians should *never assume* inspections by the state agencies are accurate. *Trust but verify!*

After the first announced visit to get to know the foster caregivers and to establish a good working relationship, on later visits we typically show-up *unannounced* to see the children. Most foster caregivers do not like surprises! We feel it is our duty to find out what the real circumstances are like with the children and their environment. The GAL Program provides a selection of children's gifts, donated by charitable organizations, like *The Guardian ad Litem Foundation*, which we use to gain children's trust so they will be more open with us during visits (it is a *little bribe*). We also speak to the children privately to better understand what is *really happening* at their foster home.

Schoolteachers usually understand more about the children than biological or foster parents recognize; that's because they see them more during daytime hours than anyone else. In addition, many foster care providers have full or part-time jobs. Interviewing schoolteachers and counselors provides a very valuable source of in depth information, especially since my partner was an educator for 40 years, and she relates to the teachers' everyday challenges. We also see the children at their school *privately*, since they might be afraid to tell us the complete truth at the foster caregiver home. We typically prepare a list of key topics or questions in advance of these meetings.

In general, foster homes are clean, provide good food, and are safe environments for the children under their care. *Some are too good!* What do we mean by that? If the foster care home and environment happens to be much better than the biological parent's homes, why would they want to go back home? This is especially true where the children are about 5-7 years or older, where "bonding" between parents and the children is borderline, or does not exist at all. If their foster parents provide better food, nicer clothes, a private bedroom, their own TV, maybe a swimming pool, why would any child want to return to their parent's pandemonium?

Bonding is partly a subjective judgment call: do the children *naturally hug* when they meet mom and dad, with clear signs of real attachment, or not? Are the children positively or negatively upset, before and after parental meetings? Much depends on the age of the children. Normal babies at about age 1-3 years are spontaneous in showing affection. Parents and children can often "fake it" during meetings. GALs need to see them together for at least 3-4 visitations to make a reasonable determination.

We had a case where mom and dad played affectionately with the baby and took photos, *when supervised*. Afterward, when supervised visits were no longer required, and they were out of this "fish bowl," they skipped on their baby's basic requirements to buy illegal drugs, and fought each other over their drug and alcohol habits. A severe addict is *out-of-control*; they will do whatever it takes to get their indispensable "fix."

Very few foster caregivers are "bad apples." Some take in 4-7 children or more partly because of the money. Florida generally pays the foster care providers about $400 or more per child each month. Medical foster care gets additional compensation since they are professionals or nurses, and they must care for extremely sick or handicapped children. That is not much compensation considering the cost of living these days. Though, if foster care parents skip on the children's food, clothing and other essentials, they can make a nice profit (dirty money). If GAL suspects that might be happening, especially any mistreatment of the children, we gather evidence, and then raise bright red flags. Once we have enough facts, we will report it to our supervisor or case coordinator, the case manager, and ultimately to the director and to the court, if that becomes necessary. We *never* tolerate any mistreatment of "our children."

**"Johnnie-come-lately"**

Source Gay Courter: *I Speak for This Child* (Condensed for this book).

The relative who had been stuck with the infant turned her over to foster care. Her first foster mother adored the child and immediately applied to adopt her. However, as soon as the process began, the missing natural mother showed up—or at least her attorney made a court appearance—and claimed the mother wanted her baby back.

Visitations were begun, with the mother only showing up for one out of five appointments, and then demonstrating very little interest in the child, who clung to her foster mother because *she did not know her real mother* (emphasis mine). Finally, when the mother did not appear for two court hearings, termination of parental rights (TPR) procedures began in preparation for the adoption.

At the last minute, a grandmother demanded custody of her granddaughter, and DCF changed the child's plan from adoption, to placement with a relative. My mother's diligent investigation of this grandmother revealed she had given up three of her children to foster care and had lied about several other essential matters. After more than a year of constant prodding by the Guardian ad Litem, finally her foster family, the only family she had ever known, adopted this little girl.

## Foster Care Graduates

Source: *"Raised by the Courts,"* by retired Judge Irene Sullivan (Condensed for this book)

There are, on average, about 5-6 child cases *available* per Guardian ad Litem *volunteer*. Why don't these tragic cases have more support? Part of the reason is that the state budgets have insufficient funds for case managers, supervisors, foster care homes, therapy sessions, other medical special needs and legal services. Another reason is that we need more volunteers that can really make a difference in the lives of these precious children. Greater support for the Court Appointed Special Advocates (CASA), or "Guardian ad Litem" volunteers could *save taxpayers a lot* of money, by reducing crime rates of adolescent youth that in future years feed our prisons.

Nationwide, about 5% of *all* children experience some form of the juvenile justice system. If that is true, then 95% are okay, right? *No, that is false!* Within that 5% an estimate 100,000 kids are in jails temporarily. According to the Justice Police Institute, Washington, D. C., it costs the taxpayer $240 per day for each youth in jail. (That is more costly than a five-star hotel in most major cities). In 2010, about one percent of the entire population in America (3.1 million out of 310 million citizens) were incarcerated; that is about five times more than Western Europe.

Part of the reason for this disparity is that the EU is a far *more socialistic* society where troubled youth are considered: "dependent" or "neglected," and then child welfare completely takes over the situation. In contrast, about one million teens are locked-up part of the time, each year in America. Child *neglect* represents about 60% of all cases in Florida. Nearly 85% of people in prisons come from the 50% of those who were once in foster care. Most "professional" foster care providers are, in our experiences, good caregivers. The primary cause of child neglect and abuse, which leads to foster care, *is clearly illegal drug addiction by their parents.*

## Aging Out of Foster Care

Sadly, about 20,000 youth "age out" of foster care, in Florida, after reaching the legal age of 18 years, each year." The age limit has been increased to 21 years recently. (See: *Network on Transition to Adulthood*). Regrettably, these young adults age-out of foster homes when they reach "legal age," without sufficient support systems to survive in the real world. If young adults are dumped on our streets, without a home, without sufficient education, without job skills, his/her sense of hopelessness can (will) become huge. Does anyone wonder why our youth turn to alcohol, drugs, sex and crime in order to cope with life?

The most recent federal study, completed before 2001 (which needs updating), found that two years after leaving the [CASA/GAL] system, almost half (<50%) of the young people who "age out" of foster care had NOT completed high school, and more than half (>50%) were NOT employed. About 40% of these foster care "graduates" had become a [significant] "cost to the community" (on either welfare or prison rolls) and only 17% were completely self-supporting. (Source: *Reversing the Failure of the Foster Care System" Harvard Woman's Law Journal, 2004).*

These authors believe it is clearly *bogus economics* and a foolish tax choice, not to invest in our youth's education and vocational job training, *before* being tossed out of foster care; otherwise, unskilled youth will ultimately become a greater burden to society. Why can't we nip this problem earlier? Can't we provide skills and training (plumbers, electricians, carpenters, landscapers, etc.)? If we do not do that, the cost to society, not merely in taxes, but in serious crime, will become far greater in future years.

We must help our troubled youth, who have deep scars from parental neglect or worse (sexual, physical and psychological abuse), so that they can become meaningful members of society, with a sense of self-esteem and good ethical values.

Guardians cannot discuss a subject that is critically missing in most of our cases because it is not "Politically Correct" and forbidden by the government. GALs cannot discuss spirituality or faith with families and children. Yet the facts show that faith-based education and religious foster care systems have a much better results with our youth.

## Transitioning from Foster Care

Source: *Ready for Life* (Condensed for this book)

For young adults that have aged out of foster care, many of them start making major life decisions starting at an unusually young age. They face more of those decisions than ever at the age of 18. "What do we do now that we have attained something that most of us have been dreaming about for years... control over our own lives?"

This generation is offered more support than ever before, they have many choices, they can finish high school, get a GED, attend college, learn a trade, go to work, so many decisions. These are more than decisions however, they are incredible opportunities and they often have second, and third chances to prove themselves, to prove wrong the stigmas that follow "foster kids" around. They are also incredible responsibilities for someone so newly on their own often without much guidance or support.

All of these choices require a fulltime commitment, we are expected to "jump in" 100% hoping that we've made the right decision for ourselves based on our limited experiences of what we might want or need at age 18, because after all, many of us only have one shot at getting it right. We all want to believe in ourselves, to make something of ourselves, to be better than what we were born to, to do better than what we were raised with, to show everyone who told us we couldn't.

We have this fire in the beginning, we idealize, we dream about succeeding, we see the path that will take us there, but it is hard to envision the many obstacles that will come between us, and our goals. The twists and turns in our paths, the many detours on the road of life makes it easy to get discouraged, to lose sight of the end of that road, to let old doubts back in, to wonder if we were really meant for something better.

When we are "in" (in state care) we have people(case workers, foster parents, Guardian ad Litem, and mentors) who recognize and are constantly fighting these kinds of self-defeating thought patterns that are pretty typical for someone who has experienced the things that we have. What many do not realize is that, when we are left to our own devices, that is when these doubts will hit the hardest and this is when most of our support services has dropped off just when we need it the most!

I am so thankful that I am working with Ready for Life whose mission is to engage the youth and our community to support youth at this critical time. Youth aging out of foster care are a population that for so long has been ignored. We need to continue to make strides in this area, so that youth are supported, connected and feel like someone cares. End.

The author of this book was a foster care child in the early 1940s, and I can tell you from direct experience, that except for the *grace of God*, I could have become one of those lost statistics. Instead, I had an opportunity to serve this country in the USAF, I learned about computer technology, became an executive for a consulting company, and later established my own firm. I retired at age 55, volunteered at the VA Hospice, and now, together with my spouse of 50 years, we were active members of *Guardian ad Litem*.

***Just one new Guardian can change a child's life forever!***

# DRUGS, SEX & VIOLENCE

These GALs thought that when we relocated to Florida, we would be moving to a more conservative state and city compared to "progressive an liberal" NYC, Boston and San Francisco—*it was not so*. Our experience has been that law breakers with multiple DUI's, VOP, and arrests for possession or selling illegal drugs, and cases of domestic violence, get out of jail with essentially a slap on the wrist, like a few days' worth of community service. These offenders later commit other, far more serious crimes.

Illegal drugs, especially "pill mills" in 90% of our cases were the *major cause* of domestic violence, which ultimately led to child neglect and abuse by parents. Incredible is the fact that pill pushers were waiting outside of PAR (where addicts to go for random urine analysis). It was an ideal place to find vulnerable clients for their product.

Addicted juveniles and adults *must* be constrained in a treatment facility where they get professional help. The ability of addicts to walk out of treatment clinics, based on their "individual legal rights" is senseless—*it does not work*. It is a waste of time and taxpayer funds. How many Hollywood stars went back to their old addictive habits, after a few weeks of treatment? *Bad habits can only be replaced with good habits.*

**A baby is born addicted to drugs about once an hour, study says**
By Karen Kaplan, Los Angeles Times (Condensed for this book)

The proportion of pregnant women who are addicted to opiates increased nearly *fivefold* between 2000 and 2009. Accordingly, the proportion of babies born addicted to the drugs who experience withdrawal after birth nearly tripled during the same period.

These calculations come courtesy of researchers from the University of Michigan and the University of Pittsburgh, who reported their findings in the Journal of the American Medical Assn. After combing through hospital data compiled by the federal Agency for Healthcare Research and Quality, the team found that 3.39 out of every 1,000 babies born in an American hospital in 2009 had neonatal abstinence syndrome, up from 1.2 out of every 1,000-hospital births in 2000. That translates to 13,539 newborns in 2009 – or roughly one born per hour that year.

Neonatal abstinence syndrome, or NAS, affects babies who become addicted to drugs in utero—especially opiates—and go through withdrawal once they are living outside the womb. Symptoms include seizures and tremors, respiratory distress, vomiting and an inability to eat without becoming sick.

Treatments have not improved much in the past decade, and some babies require morphine or methadone to get over their addictions. The typical baby born with NAS winds up staying in the hospital for about 16 days before he or she can be discharged, according to the JAMA report.

The immediate cause for this spike in babies with NAS is an even larger spike in pregnant women addicted to prescription painkillers, heroin and other opiates. According to the federal data, 5.63 out of every 1,000 mothers who gave birth in a hospital in 2009 were addicted to opiates, up from 1.20 per 1,000 in 2000, the study found. *Experts estimate that*

*60% to 80% of babies exposed to heroin or methadone in utero wind up addicted themselves.*

The average cost of caring for a baby with NAS has risen from $39,400 in 2000 to $53,400 in 2009 – an increase of 35%, despite the fact that the amount of time affected infants remained in the hospital did not change over the decade. Adjusting for inflation, the total money spent to care for babies with neonatal abstinence syndrome jumped from $190 million to $720 million over that period. The share of the total tab picked up by Medicaid rose from 69% in 2000 to 78% in 2009, according to the JAMA study.

"Novel pharmacotherapy research is needed to improve maternal opiate maintenance strategies to protect the fetus from in utero withdrawal, and to reduce the incidence and severity of NAS," they write. As one hopeful sign, they mention recent findings that link two particular genes with the severity of withdrawal symptoms in newborns. Someday, doctors may be able to tailor their treatments for these babies by checking to see what versions of these (and perhaps other) genes they have.

# SEXUAL ABUSE OF CHILDREN

Interaction between a child and adult or older child, for sexual stimulation of the perpetrator is sexual abuse. Sex offenders are usually very charming persons that gain the trust of the child and family they victimize. Someone they know personally, typically sexually abuses most children. They are not usually battered or bruised and they generally do not fight back. Many cases go *unreported* to parents and authorities because of fear of consequences: negative reaction of parents, disruption of the family, personal embarrassment, and they are afraid of punishment for telling a secret.

Symptoms and effects of sexual abuse are physical injury, sleeplessness, disturbed eating habits, pelvic pain, intestinal disorders, VD infection, headaches, and back pain. Psychological symptoms include anxiety, guilt feelings, grief, nervousness, depression, sleeplessness and nightmares, feelings of shame, suicidal tendencies, and insecurity. Emotional and behavioral effects are withdrawing from friends, being easily frightened, trouble concentrating, restlessness, bedwetting, substance abuse, and fear of sex. Children (and many adults) tend to block out bad experiences.

By [Katherine Timpf](Katherine Timpf) (Condensed for this book):
These events were part of UC-Berkeley's celebration of National Condom Week.

A group of elementary and middle school students touring University of California - Berkeley last week were exposed to a man in a giant penis costume and school-sponsored sex games. "All day long, little kids were prancing by ... sex-themed games of chance, and the guy in the penis suit," student Claire said in an interview with *Campus Reform*.

Children were led through the campus quad while Berkeley students were playing "pin-the-tail on the anus" and tossing condoms through holes on a poster board meant to represent vaginas and anuses. There was also a man dressed as a giant penis handing out condoms, although not permitted to hand them to the children. These were preplanned events, as part of the school's celebration of National Condom Week.

**Exposure to Violence:** Neglected and/or abused children, ultimately become irresponsible adolescents, and abusive adults, creating a cradle-to-prison pipeline for American society. Judge Irene Sullivan, in her book, "*Raised by the Courts*" says, "Kids are violent because they experience violence." We know what works, and we know what doesn't work. We have a clear choice between building more expensive prisons later, and directly addressing the causes of this chaos now. "Family violence needs a family solution," she adds. American society has become the "incarceration nation of the world."

Studies have also persuasively demonstrated that depictions of extreme violence in video games like "*Mortal Kombat*" and "*Grand Theft Auto: Vice City*" harm youngsters' mental health, according to pediatricians who disagreed with part of a U.S. Supreme Court decision striking down a California ban on video game sales to children.

MRI images have shown that abused children and TV violent programs cause changes in brain development associated with chemical surges, causing cognitive, behavioral and emotional problems—they become the angry kids that become the *root cause* of so much of the trouble in our 21$^{st}$ century society. However, mental health experts agreed with the justices that ultimately, parents have the responsibility to vet and control what their children watch and play.

"The studies are actually very strong," said Dr. Laura Davies, a child and adolescent psychiatrist at California Pacific Medical Center in San Francisco. She had just read a paper published in the *Journal Pediatrics* that found violent videos disrupted preschoolers' sleep. Every one of us—child psychiatrists, behavioral pediatricians and regular pediatricians, see in our practices every day that when children (younger than seven) are exposed to violence and to trauma, they act out ... by biting, hitting, kicking, name-calling, wetting themselves, poor sleep, poor eating," Davies said. "Older kids act out by fighting, with academic problems, social problems, bullying, anxiety, fearfulness, withdrawal from friends."

Writing for the high court's 7-2 majority, Justice Scalia agreed with a lower court that the state of California failed to prove that depictions of "killing, maiming, dismembering or sexually assaulting an image of a human being" were sufficiently harmful to young minds to justify carving out a free speech exception solely for children. For centuries, young children have been exposed to "no shortage of gore" in Grimm's "Fairy Tales," he wrote. "Cinderella's evil stepsisters have their eyes pecked out by doves. And Hansel and Gretel (children!) kill their captor by baking her in an oven."

Davies, however, said the impact of reading Grimm's "Fairy Tales" on the page could not be compared with the visual and aural assault of a violent video: "It's much more vivid and much more traumatic," she said. On another level, though, repeatedly playing these fictional, interactive videos distorts children's concept of death, she said. "When I interview kids in my forensic practice, and they've killed somebody, they don't think the person is going to stay dead," she said. "They think that what they see on TV with these video games, with the movies, is that you kill them and you get another life."

Dina L. G. Borzekowski, an associate professor of health, behavior and society at the Johns Hopkins School of Public Health in Baltimore, said she concurred with Justice Stephen Breyer's dissent, in which he found a "compelling interest in protecting the physical and psychological well-being of minors."

As video games, more than half rated as containing violence, become increasingly sophisticated, "it is very scary to think how children and adolescents will be sold products where they can practice violence," Borzekowski said. "I think that parents can use more tools, not fewer, to guide their children in better media choices," she said. The Supreme Court decision "allows children to buy virtual boxing gloves, and yes, virtual guns." As deplorable as she finds violent videos, Borzekowski said she opposes censorship. Instead, she would limit children's exposure to them with age restrictions, much like film ratings limit at what age children can see movies depicting sex, drugs or bad language.

These GALs must add that even TV commercials are violent, with parents hitting a spouse, making dad appear silly and dumb, and they abuse the English language. They also give children false ideas, with "*you can have it all*" slogans, among others.

We had a case where foster parents allowed the children under their care to play with violent video games, and watch R-rated TV programs. It was a form of "electronic babysitting," that gave them relief from their caregiver responsibilities. When we visited and spoke to these children, we had to ask them to please shut off the game and listen to us. They reluctantly did so, but went back to their game immediately afterward. They later became abusive brothers to each other, and classmates in school. They required intervention by therapists to break their violent anti-social behaviors.

Why do we experience so much sex and violence? Because this TV, games and movie rubbish appeals to the lowest common dominator, the masses, and producers say it improves ratings. It certainly does improve ratings, and sells more "things," that most of us do not need. (See Appendix on: *Violent Video Games* study by Ohio University)

## Death of Outrage

"Interestingly, prosperity actually depends upon good morals. When lying, cheating, manipulation, lack of moral discipline, and personal irresponsibility become commonplace, then national economies will decline." Mr. Bennett, former Secretary of Education and Drug Czar wrote in his book, *The Death of Outrage*,

"A society that produces street predators and white-collar criminals has to pay for prison cells. A society in which drug use is rampant must pay for drug treatment centers. The breakup of families means many more foster homes and lower high school graduation rates. ... Just as there are enormous financial benefits to moral health, there are enormous financial costs to moral collapse."

Bennett continues, "Religious congregations dismiss pastors for unethical or inappropriate private behavior, regardless of the quality of their sermons. In law enforcement, a good police commissioner will rid his department of a bigoted cop, regardless of how sterling the officer's arrest record. In the world of the military, the code of military justice demands rigid standards of personal conduct, no matter how great a soldier's prowess on the battlefield."

What Bennett was suggesting in his book is this: "The attempt to use God's forgiveness as a pretext to excuse moral wrong is a dangerous (and old) heresy known as *antinomianism*—literally 'against the law.' Essentially, it rejects the moral law as a relevant part of Christian experience. The thought that Christ's death at Golgotha, would justify licentiousness has long been considered contemptible by saints and scholars."

"Those who constantly invoke the sentiment of 'who are we to judge?' should consider the anarchy that would ensue if we adhered to this sentiment in, say, our courtrooms. Shouldn't judges judge? What would happen if those sitting on a jury decided to be 'nonjudgmental' about rapists and sex harassers, embezzlers and tax cheats? Without being 'judgmental,' Americans would never have put an end to slavery, outlawed child labor, emancipated women, or ushered in the civil rights movement.

"Forgiveness cannot be granted without admission of guilt, without an apology, without repentance. Forgiveness has become, in some societies, a synonym for lax standards and tolerance for (and acceptance of) all kinds of misbehavior."

# SOCIETAL SOLUTIONS

*"When the heart is set right, then the personal life is cultivated; when personal life is cultivated, then the family life is regulated; when family life is regulated, then national life is orderly; and when national life is orderly, then there is peace in the world."* Confucius (5th Century BC)

## Family Responsibility

Family is the natural order in any civil society in which husband and wife give themselves in love and participate, together with God, in the gift of life. Authority, stability, and a life of relationships within the family constitute the foundations for freedom, security, and fraternity within any society. The family is the community in which, from childhood, one must learn moral values, begin to honor God, and make good use of this freedom. Family life is an initiation into life in the greater society. Following the principle of subsidiary, larger communities and government should be careful not to usurp the family's prerogatives or interfere with its inner life, without due cause, like for example, clear evidence of child neglect or abuse.

## Causes of Family Disintegration

Family structures in traditional societies are usually patriarchal, ruled by the father, but too often matriarchal, ruled by the mother, especially in 73% of African-American families. Whichever is the case, there should be only one ruler in any family, as there is only one captain of a ship. Divorced or unmarried single parents are one of the major causes of disintegration of the family structure. This is especially true when the father or mother abandons his or her responsibility to each other and to the children.

A God-centered civilization, that has freedom, is *usually* family-oriented, teaches its children early moral values, demands individual responsibility, and promotes literacy. That kind of free society produces compassionate, productive, responsible individuals, who exemplify *"a cult of life."* It is similar to a pyramid, where faith in God is at the pinnacle, followed by the family with respect for parents, moral values, and a sense of personal responsibility for one's acts. Everything that is good flows from Freedom, Faith and Family. Conversely, a secular nation, or fanatical fundamentalist religious society, often leads to dysfunctional families, deterioration of human values, lack of individual responsibility, and eventually, disintegration of the culture—*"a cult of death."*

Dysfunctional parents often produce impaired children. This situation often leads to neglected or abused grandchildren as well. Dysfunction can become an endless cycle, similar to a cancer that spreads, incessantly. Children (and immature adults) today have an "instant gratification," or "me first" attitude. Who were their key role models?

Nevertheless, we have seen numerous examples of fantastic, wonderful children who have grown up in dysfunctional families, under disadvantaged circumstances, and yet, somehow they became righteous, responsible adults, even great leaders. Who or what saved them from that crisis. We portray it as "Three Pillars for Survival:" (1) At least one loving parent who wants what is good for their child; (2) A balanced education; and (3) A moral foundation with Jewish, Christian or Islamic faiths. If one pillar is broken, the child usually goes under in *any* society. How many public schools teach morality?

Minority prejudice, earlier economic conditions, and social climate caused these *worst of times*, some will argue. Yet a few generations ago, other ethnic groups were minorities—Asians, Irish, Italians, Germans, Jews, and now Hispanics are the new generation of minorities. These 2$^{nd}$ generation immigrants also experienced significant economic hardships, like the Great Depression, severe environmental conditions (urban squalor), and appalling discrimination. Yet, legions have succeeded. Let's face it, the *fundamental roots* of our societal crises are caused by three factors: (1) abdication of parental responsibility, (2) faulty education, and (3) *most importantly*, lack of trust in God.

## Responsibility of Parents

> *Children need love, especially when they don't deserve it.*
> —Harold S. Hulbert

The fecundity of conjugal love is not solely for the procreation of children, but must extend to their moral education and their spiritual formation. Any two consenting adults can produce children; it happens by the tens-of-thousands, every day, throughout the world. Unfortunately, too many of these kids are born in underdeveloped poor countries, where poverty and disease are widespread, and formal education does not exist. The definition of parenting is not merely procreation, as animals do; it is about nurturing, supporting and educating children. Otherwise, it is simply *irresponsible sex*.

Daycare has become a place where parents "dispose" their children, thus avoiding parental responsibilities, most of the day. (However, some poor single parents have to work and they have no other choice). If a family earns enough to pay the essential bills, the mother should stay at home for at least 2-3 years, to provide that *vital nurturing* which every infant needs. There is no excuse for higher income parents to turn their children over to Daycare providers, so that they can explore a "profession."

We had a case where the parents sent their five children, including one six-month infant to Daycare, from about 7 AM to 7 PM, every weekday. She had a serious addiction problem. The Case Manager arranged this *free* childcare service, paid by government Head Start. Mom had no job and spent most of her day watching TV soap operas.

Many families, especially minority groups, only have a single parent today. The parent must work, and thus spends less quality time with their children. Earlier generations of parents experienced similar or greater economic challenges, yet they spent more time with their children. Ethnic communities prior to the late 1960's, were tightly integrated where everyone knew each other and looked after the kids on the block. Today, the once venerated family and multi-ethnic cultural communities are rapidly disintegrating.

The effect of these trends are obvious everywhere: children lack respect for their parents; moral values have declined; teenage-pregnancy is on the rise; an appalling culture of drugs is upon us; and adolescent crime has increased at an alarming rate. Nevertheless, many ethnic families, Hispanics, Asians, and Jews, for example, still pull together to help each other. Hispanic families for example, will take in an orphaned child and raise them as if they were blood brothers or sisters. About 15% of the population of the United States are *legal* Hispanics (not counting the estimate 12 million undocumented Latinos), and future demographics are changing rapidly.

The role of parents in education is of such great importance that it is almost impossible to provide an adequate substitute. The right and duty of parents to educate their children is *"a primordial and inalienable right."* Parents must regard their progeny as children of God and respect them as human persons. Parents have the first responsibility for the basic education of their children at home. They bear witness to this responsibility first by creating a home environment where security, tenderness, forgiveness, respect, trustworthiness and selfless service are the rule.

If all children are born innocent, precious, and loveable, then what is it that caused so many of these "beautiful flowers in God's garden," to become delinquents, drug addicts, sexually permissive, and amoral? Is this learned behavior? *Of course it is!* Many did not learn basic moral principles from their parents. How many of these originally good children had dysfunctional parents, or grew up in a faithless family? Who were their early role models? What kind of friends did they grow up with in their teen years? Were their childhood experiences secure, positive and supportive, or were they insecure, negative and indifferent.

Consider our analogy from nature: without good earth, without rain and sunshine, and without cultivation, nothing flourishes. Gardens need to be cultivated until roots of the flowers have grown deeper and are well established. Innocent children resemble beautiful flowers of every type and variety, and they too require constant nurturing in a loving family, until their roots are fully developed. The nature of a flower is to blossom; and the radiance of its colors and smells can be like God's paradise. Remember this truism: the neglected or abused child of the today will become the primary source of crime, terrorism and misery in the future.

One of the key problems is this: how can dysfunctional parents teach their children anything? What kind of role model will they be? If that is the actual situation, then other family members, State Social Services authorities, and ultimately the Church, must play a much greater role. If the parents lack adequate Christian instruction, how can one expect them to teach their children about Christ? In many cases, *both* the parents and their children will need fundamental religious instruction.

According to a recent US Department of Commerce survey, about 17% of the population, age 25 and older, lack a high school diploma; 24% have a college degree, and 8% earned graduate degrees. Interestingly, those *without* a high school diploma only earned $16,124 per year; those with a high school diploma earned $22,895; the BA/BS degree persons earned $40,478; and the advanced degree group earned $63,229 (all are average salaries). These statistics, by themselves, should convince parents and teenagers that *a good education really pays.*

## Responsibility of Children

> *There are no illegitimate children, only illegitimate parents.*
> —Leon Yankwich

The respect of children, for the father and mother, is nourished by the natural affection born of the bond uniting them. It is required of God's fifth commandment (Ex 20:12). Respect for parents (filial piety) derives from gratitude toward those who, by the gift of life, their love and work, have brought their children into the world and enabled them to grow in stature, wisdom and grace. Through your parents, you were born; what can you give back to them that compares to their gift of life to you?

As long as a child lives at home with his/her parents, the child should obey the parents in all that is reasonable, when it is for his/her good or that of the family. However, if a child is convinced in conscience that it would be morally wrong to obey a particular order, he/she must not do so. Obedience toward parents ceases with the emancipation (defined as reaching the legal age and living responsibly alone) of the children, not so respect (for parents), which is *always* owed to them.

Some young adults today, think that they need not respect and obey their parents. "I'm not a child anymore; I'm an adult, and you can't tell me what to do," they typically say. Nevertheless, while this young adult lives in their parents' house, they must continue to follow all reasonable rules and guidelines of the mother and father, under their roof, and always have good manners and honor for those who gave them life, no matter how mature and educated they think they are.

Another typical expression by some of today's adolescents and young adults is this: "I'm bored!" "Let's go to the movies," or "shopping at the Mall." Our response is simple: Boredom is *within* you; movies, TV, or other events may provide a temporary diversion, but it will not last. The solution is to do something useful, or better yet, do something for someone else. Avoid thinking about *your* wants (which usually are not needs). Read a book; do work around the home, or better yet, do a work of charity; pray for guidance, and then, *listen to the voice within.*

## Responsibility of Society

Society is a group or assembly of persons bound together naturally (as living entities) by a principle of unity that goes beyond each of them individually. By means of society, each man and woman becomes "heirs" and receives certain "talents" that enrich his or her identity, whose fruits they should develop.

Most humans need to live in a society, where through the exchange and dialogue with others, and mutual service with their brethren, they can develop their full potential. Love of neighbor is also *inseparable* from love of God. Human society cannot be well ordered or prosperous unless it has some people invested with legitimate authority to preserve its institutions, who devote themselves to care for the common good of all. Members of a society rightly owe loyalty to the communities of which they are a part, and should respect those *just* legal authorities who have charge of the common good. Society should always promote the exercise of all good virtues.

States have no permanent alliances, only permanent self-interests. The state must be concerned foremost about the security, health and welfare of its citizens. It should promote the "common good" of the society, by creating and enforcing the *rule of just laws*, while always respecting the dignity of each person. Authority of the state does not derive its moral legitimacy from itself; it must act for the common good of all as a "moral force" based on freedom and responsibility.

The *good of the individual person* should be the principle, subject, and the end goal of all social institutions. Excessive intervention by the state can threaten personal freedoms, and must be avoided. Regimes whose nature is contrary to "natural law," to public order, and to the basic rights of citizens cannot achieve the common good. Any state that views persons as simple "means to some end" will engender unjust political and economic structures that can make moral conduct difficult, if not impossible. We have seen many examples of evil of states from earlier Nazism and Communism tyrants.

## American Bill of Rights

Freedom *of* Religion *doesn't* mean separation of God *from* life and society);

Freedom *of* Speech (does not mean accepting TV pollution into your home).

Freedom *of* the Press (does not mean inventing news and false reporting).

Legal Rights *for* the accused (does not mean criminals have more legal rights than victims).

Right *of* Fair Trial (does not mean abusing the justice system for advantage).

Our Civil Rights were established for American citizens, *not for foreigners and terrorists.*

What is missing from these freedoms? Where are **Children's rights?** Women today have equal rights with men. Shouldn't there be a **Constitutional amendment** giving basic human rights to every child, no matter their age? Children should clearly have a right to a safe, permanent, and healthy life.

Nonetheless, Freedom for freedoms sake is foolish! You do not have freedom to get drunk and hurt someone. You can't drive without a license. You can't have sex with a minor child. Individual "rights" are *balanced* against the rights of the entire society.

Who is responsible for teaching children morality? Is it the judge's role to get involved in analyzing children's behavior? A judge's role is (should be) interpretation of existing laws against the facts of the case. Parents in the home have the **primary** responsibility to teach morality. Parents have an *obligation* to provide protection, structure and support for children, until they reach the legal age. Even when they become adults, if they continue to live under your roof and depend on you for their welfare, the parents are in charge. They *think* they are adults, but cannot always make wise, save choices. Teens and young adults have to learn to deal with successes and failures, praise and rejection, happiness and disappointment, and take responsibility for choices and the *consequences*.

## Custody Contests

If you are not experienced or knowledgeable about what goes on in high-conflict divorces and child custody cases, you may want to familiarize yourself with what might come your way. The following is a list of typical "dirty tricks" used in custody cases:

- Clean out the bank account or safety deposit box of the partner.

- Claim very limited income to evade alimony by avoiding bank accounts.

- Run-up the account balances on credit cards of the former partner.

- Engage in parental alienation or otherwise speaking poorly in front of the children and other family members and friends.

- Move unannounced out of state, taking your children with you, and cutting off all contact, claiming it is for the *"best interest of the children."*

- File a petition and restraining order to get you kicked out of your own home and restricted from even coming onto the property at any time.

- Spread nasty rumors and speak poorly about you in front of mutual friends.

- Withhold or interfere with your visitation rights (custodial interference).

- File motions and use delay tactics to tie you up in court and drain your finances.

- Falsely claim physical or sexual abuse against you or the children.

- Get a restraining order against you based on various false allegations.

- Force you to move out of the house through harassment and coercion, and then petition the court claiming you have *"abandoned the family."*

- Involve family members, friends, or others in malicious actions against you.

- Deny, restrict, or interfere with private mail and telephone access to the children.

- Interfere with your participating in your child's school and other activities.

- Use your mutual or, unsuspecting "friends" to get inside information to use against you in court. Trying to get the children to be spies against you.

These tactics are used with alarming frequency and effectiveness to frustrate, outmaneuver, and obtain a legal upper hand, and wear the targeted parent down. Sadly, it is becoming more commonplace for *some* unscrupulous attorneys to recommend one or more of these tactics to their clients because it gives them a decided advantage and almost guarantees victory in court (and greater attorney fees). For instance, if your ex-partner can convince the courts that you have physically abused her or your child, she gains a tremendous advantage over you in all further proceedings. The father gets labeled as a *"violent offender,"* a person for whom judges have limitless disdain, and they will not hesitate to grant the false accuser whatever they want.

Unfortunately, even when you are successful in turning away these charges and win, perception becomes reality. It becomes reality to "friends;" a stain that is hard to remove. It is *imperative* that you remain the calm, rational person with your ex-partner. The less you do to provoke conflict the better off you will be in the end. You never want to be responsible for a situation getting out of control, as it will be the foundation for much heartache later. *Try praying for your ex-partner.*

# ADOPTION PROCESS

*An Adoption Tale* tells of two parents who dream about a baby and then travel to a faraway place to bring their baby girl home. When they are all home together, they celebrate being a family. This book talks about foster parents—"the kind people who had taken care of her"—and the biological mother—"you grew like a flower in another lady's tummy"—as important parts of the journey.

Adoption sounds like a quick remedy. The final papers are signed, and everyone lives happily ever after. Adoptive parents can become fed up, particularly with teenage behaviors, and turn the kids back to the state system. The state has to accept them. (They think they are getting a new pair of shoes and can return them). Then we are stuck with older kids who usually take this next failure so hard emotionally they might be worse off than before, and will probably spend the rest of their minority life in foster care. Adoption is a *chance*, maybe a slight one. Why should we second-guess it and deny them this little window of opportunity? There is a tremendous amount of work by the ECA, CM, GAL, and special lawyers, putting one of these adoptions together.

For example, these GALs were involved in the adoption of two sisters. Everything looked great. Reports we got back from "Courtesy GAL" visits were that everything is "fine and dandy." Our supervisor told us, "don't rock the boat," by probing too much. "Leave it to the Adoption CM; she's the 'expert' and knows what's happening."

We accepted this for about six months. Suddenly, the whole adoption process began to unravel, at the last minute. The adopting parents got "cold feet." They wanted one girl, but not her troubled sister. We demanded that the siblings remain together; it was a "matched pair of shoes." Why were they suddenly changing their minds? What was the truth? What was really happening?

The truth was that the adopting parents, bought a new, bigger home, and were running "a foster care business" to pay the mortgage (they had no other source of income). The license was for five kids, but because of serious foster home shortages, they had 7-9 children. Seven kids times over $450 (average) each per month, is $3,150, which pays the mortgage and other goodies. These troubled foster sisters would definitely interfere with their foster business.

We later learned that these sisters were forced to sleep three children to one bed, in a Recreational Vehicle, while home construction was being completed. These Guardians protested, but lacked sufficient proof to support our foster business scheme theory. Foster care is a separate organization, not connected with GAL or CASA. Besides, they were outside our court's jurisdiction.

The adoption failed! These sisters went to a foster group home, with fifty strangers in a major city. *They were devastated!* We were the only connecting link with their future. We visited them almost twice each month, although it was about 50 miles roundtrip.

They received good therapy from capable professionals, but the psychiatrist was "experimenting" with psychotropic meds. He reduced their meds too soon, which caused serious social problems. One of the troubled sisters became more aggressive. When harassed by her peers, she physically attacked the other child. The psychiatrist answer was to expel her from the group home, and put her in a mental institution.

These GALs sent off loud alarms to *everyone*. We did not give a crap about the chain-of-command processes. We demanded action for "our girls." Finally, about a week later, Eckerd Community Alternatives (ECA) found a "therapeutic foster mom" who would accept these sisters. They lucked out. She happened to be an excellent choice for them.

What is next? Will the process continue? Where is that so-called "expert" Adoption CM? She knew or should have known that the adoption process was not really working. She should have alerted all of us that it was not going to happen.

We attended a Status Review hearing. The judge knew about the disaster. These GALs asked the Adopting CM, at the hearing, "When can we expect the essential Children's Study to be finalized? When can we expect the girl's pictures in the state's Adoption Photo Gallery?" We receive typical B.S. answers: "Well, documentation is in process," you know we have to update our review. We hope to complete the paperwork in about sixty days."

Six months later, *nothing was completed*. We did not win any points by pointing out her screw-ups. Our supervisor said to me, "Robert, try to be a nice guy."

"I'm not in this volunteer work to win 'a damn personality contest.' I didn't give a crap about being a 'nice guy.'" At this stage. *I was really pissed!*

Miriam and I prayed for these girls, endlessly. All seemed to be lost. It was a terrible tragedy. He was our only hope. ECA assigned a new Adoption CM to the case. We asked to have a coffee meeting away from her office, ASAP. We seemed to "click" immediately. She fully understood the details of the case, and was a very sincere person—*she was a woman of action!*

A few weeks later, the kid's photos were in the Adoption Photo Gallery. The children's Report was completed. Dozens of families were interested in adopting these beautiful sisters. The Adopting CM introduced us to three of the "most likely" candidates.

Finally, about three months later we agreed that the younger, more active, educated married couple were probably "the best choice." The adoption process was in full gear. All required paperwork took additional months. Next, we observed the family together with the sisters during a two-month period. It was a perfect match; *a match made in heaven*. God has His way of turning evil into goodness.

## I Speak for this Child

Author, Courter, Gay (Condensed for this book)

"Our federal funding structure actually hinders the resolution of foster care cases. As long as we spend more to reimburse agencies for maintaining children in foster homes and do not offer social services to either repair the family relationships quickly or facilitate adoptions, children will wither in transient homes. Time is of the essence when it comes to moving children. Intervention in a family crisis should be a team effort. First, the child should be in the home, if possible, and services given to that family. If that fails—or if the child is in jeopardy—a plan that considers intervention with constant monitoring should be attempted.

"Goals must be set, and a timeline established. A year-old baby living apart from her drug-addicted mother for six months has been out of her home for half her life. A three-year-old in a foster home for a year has spent one-third of his life attached to another family. Anyone who works with these children should hear the clock ticking loudly. Procedures must be speeded up accordingly. Children cannot be allowed to languish just because they are "safe" for the moment.

"However, in order to terminate parental rights the state must prove by *clear and convincing evidence* that the parent is unfit and that it is in the best interests of the child to end that relationship. In Florida, we must demonstrate that the child was adjudicated dependent, a performance agreement was offered to the parent, and that the parents failed to *substantially* comply with the agreement for reasons other than lack of financial resources or failure of ECA to make reasonable efforts to reunify the family. In addition, the court must then determine that the termination is in the *manifest best interests of the child.*

"Judges are very reluctant to bear the responsibility for severing a family forever. A 1991 Florida ruling (Padgett v. Dept. of HRS, now known as DCF) stated: that while a parent's interest in maintaining parental ties is essential, the child's entitlement to be free of physical and emotional violence is more so, and the state has a compelling interest in protecting all citizens, especially a child, against the clear threat of abuse, neglect, and death. We must include emotional abuse and neglect in this ruling. Once and for all the judiciary must discard the old maxim that whoever '*begets them gets them.*'"

**Lessons Learned:** Do not let bureaucratic red tape cause you to become discouraged; remember it is God's innocent children you are dealing with. Do not let administrative B.S. allow the adopting parents to become discouraged; nothing is ever 100% sure. They have to have faith. Adopted children, by a non-relative in Florida, receive financial assistance for each child until age eighteen, including free college within the state.

## Adoption Interviews

A social worker will interview you several times. The interviews help you develop a relationship with your social worker that will enable him or her to better understand your family and assist you with an appropriate placement. You will discuss the topics covered in the home study report (see below). You will likely be asked to give examples of your experiences with children, your important relationships, your approach to parenting, and how you handle stress and experiences of crisis or loss, including discussions about infertility, which is a topic of concern for many adoptive families. You and your social worker will discuss what age of child would best fit in your family, and other important characteristics you would be willing to accept in a child. Again, this should be both a self-reflective process and a time to educate yourself about issues with which you may not yet be familiar. With couples, some agency workers conduct all of the interviews with both prospective parents together. Others will conduct both joint and individual interviews. If families have adult children living outside the home, they also may be interviewed during this process. It is important to be honest with the social worker and yourself about your own strengths and limitations.

## Typical Adoptive Parents Interview by these GALs

When did you begin to care for these children?

What problems did you initially experience as caregivers?

Were they born addicted to drugs?

Are the babies developmentally on target for their age?

Who is the doctor? What is the doctor's latest report on them?

How did you handle these problems/challenges?

Did the mother or father of the children provide material, emotional, financial support?

How many times did the parents visit? When was the last visit?

How are the baby's doing lately (medically, physical, emotionally)?

Are all their shot records available? Show us the records.

What is your relationship and feelings about the mother and father?

## BEST INTERESTS OF THE CHILDREN

Observation of bonding between caregivers and babies is very important.

Why do you both want to adopt these children?

Brief inspection is done of all rooms (the Adoption CM does a full inspection).

During the adoption process, sometimes, at the very last minute, a relative shows up and demands custody of his/her children and the state again must change the child's plan from adoption to *"placement with a relative."* Investigation of this relative by these GALs revealed she had given up on two of her previous children to foster care and had lied about numerous essential matters.

We have found placement for both children. So, what is the big deal with *some* state bureaucratic organizations? *It could be that it wasn't their idea!* It may not have been done in the right order according to bureaucratic rules. Surely, they would not deny children a home because of bureaucratic rules, would they? *Not if GALs can help it!*

Almost a year of court appearances by the CM and Guardian ad Litem, after lots of bureaucratic nonsense, finally these children were officially adopted by the foster family; *the only family they had ever known.*

# HOME STUDIES

Home studies primarily serve to ensure that the home offers a safe environment for a child or children and meets State standards (e.g., working smoke alarms, safe storage of firearms, clean water and swimming pools, and adequate space and beds for each child). The home should be free from basic hazards and offer a child-friendly environment. For example, poisons and household cleaners should be in cupboards with childproof locks, window drape cords should not hang within reach, firearms should be inaccessible to children. Some States require an inspection from local health and fire departments in addition to the visitation by the Case Manager.

Generally, the CM is required to view all areas of the house or apartment, including children's sleep area, the basement, and the backyard. They will be looking for how you plan to accommodate a family member. CM's are not inspecting housekeeping standards. A certain level of order is necessary, but some family clutter is generally expected. A comfortable, child-friendly environment is what is expected.

### Judge clamps down on DCF Home Study

Miami Herald, by Carol Marbin Miller (Condensed for this book)

Reeling from the brutal death of a 2-year-old boy he was entrusted to protect, Miami-Dade Circuit Judge Michael A. Hanzman is peeling away much of the authority state child welfare officials normally enjoy in his courtroom—and taking more matters into his own hands. Hanzman had agreed to allow 28-year-old Angel Luis Villegas to care for his 2-year-old son, Jayden Villegas-Morales, after administrators with the Department of Children & Families (DCF) assured him Villegas had passed a "home study" designed to gauge his fitness as a parent. Jayden had been taken from his mother's custody on June 18 after Lourdes Morales was charged with child abuse.

A month later, Jayden was dead. Villegas told Miami-Dade police he "became frustrated" with the little boy, who had been vomiting for much of the day on July 17, and threw the child, striking his head against a wall, a police report says.

Though DCF had declared Villegas' home study to be "positive," it included a handful of facts that some children's advocates call troubling: Villegas was unemployed, living in a one-bedroom home with eight other children. He had been repeatedly accused of domestic violence and had admitted to child-welfare authorities that he had "an anger issue." Investigators also documented alleged marijuana use in front of the children, the presence of cockroaches in the home and instances where children were hemmed up in dirty diapers. ...

"The fact remains," Hanzman wrote, "that these initial home studies, the one here being no exception, are typically expedited—or some would say rushed—so as to be available at a shelter hearing" that must occur within 24 hours of a child's removal from his or her parents. "And for reasons not always due to 'fault' on the part of the department, some have proven unreliable."

Hanzman's solution: He will now hold full-blown hearings before approving a caregiver DCF recommends each time a child is placed in the department's custody. He also will require DCF to provide significantly more information on each family's history with the department. "In each case," Hanzman wrote, "the party advocating the placement shall present evidence sufficient to establish—to the Court's satisfaction—that the putative caretaker will provide the child a secure, safe environment. Absent such a showing, the parties are forewarned that the child will be placed—or remain—in a licensed [foster] care facility."...

Long troubled, the Department of Children and Families (DCF) has faced particularly withering criticism recently in the wake of a deadly summer that claimed seven young lives. Since May, seven youngsters who had been the subject of at least one investigation by DCF died of abuse or neglect at the hands of a parent or caregiver.

[The judge concluded:] "These cases should no doubt be investigated so the cause of whatever mistakes, if any, [that were] made are identified and measures are taken to reduce the risk of repetition. There is no excuse for allowing a child to remain in—or to be placed in—what is known, or reasonably should be known, to be a dangerous custodial arrangement, and a single death or injury resulting from such a reckless decision is one too many."

***David Wilkins, Florida's top child welfare and social services administrator, resigned amid an escalating scandal over the recent deaths of four small children who with a history of involvement with child-abuse investigators.***

## Our Home Study Experience

These GALs experienced comparable Home Study debacles, but we fought the battle to demonstrate that the particular home study was a sham. In our particular case, we convinced the father to allowed us to take pictures of "his many improvements," using our cell phone, which clearly established that his home was unsanitary and unsafe for his child—*and for himself.* There were broken windows, storage rooms without doors, dangerous chemicals, and bugs everywhere.

The CM disagreed with us and sent the supervisor who did her own inspection in front of us. She stated, **"We have seen worse—and they all have passed inspection."**

We were flabbergasted! How many children are in danger because of her attitude? It was a "management power-play," an arrogant response from one of those recently promoted CMs, which effectively stated, "Who are you to dare overrule my home study?" Not only was the home unsafe, the rest of the Home Study report contained numerous errors of fact and omissions concerning the parent's past history. What was missing in the report was the *fact* that he's a "deadbeat" father to five other children. The father had no bank accounts, so enforcement officials could not attach his earnings.

These GALs complained to higher management. Instead of backing us, however, our supervisor had to see it for herself, since we were accusing "upper management" of incompetence. Her *announced* visit gave dad an opportunity to "clean up his act." Nevertheless, we were determined not to expose "our child" to impending danger.

We have experienced other official Home Studies where someone overlooked the obvious: lack of hygiene, such as dirty diapers on the floor; kitchen cabinets containing dangerous chemicals, without child locks; broken glass; animals without vet shots; loaded guns without safety locks, etc., etc. Once we reported that a huge pet bird had chewed through the wall of the home to the supporting wood strips. Then an efficient and professional CM immediately removed the children from the home in this case.

We never assume these reports are correct. *"Trust, but verify,"* is our motto.

## Adoption Health Statements

Most agencies require prospective adoptive parents to have a recent physical exam and a statement from a physician confirming that they are essentially healthy, have a normal life expectancy, and are physically and mentally able to handle the care of a child.

If you have a medical condition that is under control (for instance, high blood pressure or diabetes that is controlled by diet and medication), you may still be approved as an adoptive family. A serious health problem that affects life expectancy may prevent approval. If your family has sought counseling or treatment for a mental health condition in the past, you may be asked to provide information or reports from those visits. Many agencies view seeking help as a sign of strength. The fact that your family obtained such help should not preclude you from adopting. However, each family's situation is unique, so check with the agencies or social workers you are considering if you have concerns.

## Income Statements

You do have to show you can manage your finances responsibly and adequately. Usually, prospective parents are asked to verify their income by providing copies of paycheck stubs, W-4 forms, or income tax forms. Many agencies also ask about savings, insurance policies (including health coverage for the adopted child), investments, and debts.

## Background Checks

All States require criminal and child abuse checks for adoptive and foster parent applicants. In many States, local, State, and Federal clearances are required.

Public and private agencies must comply with State and Federal laws and policies regarding licensing requirements and how the findings of background checks affect eligibility for adoptive parents. However, do not hesitate to talk to social workers and agencies you are considering about specific situations that might disqualify you from adopting. Agencies will consider your experiences as well as how you dealt with them, what you have learned from them, and how you would use that knowledge in parenting. Some agencies may be able to work with your family, depending on the specific incident and its resolution. If the social worker finds you to be deceptive or dishonest, however, or if the documents collected during the home study process expose inconsistencies, the agency may not approve your home study.

## Autobiographical Statement

Many adoption agencies ask prospective adoptive parents to write an autobiographical statement or story. This is, essentially, the story of your life. It helps the social worker understand your family better and assists him or her in writing the home study report (see below). If you are working with an agency that practices openness in adoption, you also may be asked to write a letter or create an album or scrapbook about your family to be shared with expectant parents who are considering placing their child for adoption, to help them choose an adoptive family. You may also be asked to prepare a similar album for children, if you are considering adopting children older than infants.

While writing about yourself may seem difficult, the exercise is to provide information about you to the agency, as well as to help you explore issues related to parenting and adoption. Some agencies have workers available to assist you with the writing. Most have a set of questions to guide you through writing your autobiography.

## References

The agency will probably ask you for names, addresses, and telephone numbers of three or four people who will serve as references for you. References help the social worker form a more complete picture of your family and support network.

If possible, references should be people who have known you for years, who have seen you in many situations, and who have visited your home and know of your interest in and involvement with children. Most agencies require that references be people who are not related to you. Good choices might include close friends, an employer, a former teacher, a coworker, a neighbor, or your pastor, minister, rabbi, or leader of your faith community (if applicable).

**Family background:** descriptions of the applicants' childhoods, how they were parented, past and current relationships with parents and siblings, key events and losses and what was learned from them

**Education/employment:** applicants' current educational levels, satisfaction with their educational achievements, any plans to further their education, as well as their employment status, history, plans, and satisfaction with their current jobs

**Relationships:** If applicants are a couple, the report may cover their history together as well as their current relationship (for example, how they make decisions, solve problems, communicate, and show affection). Single applicants will be asked about their social life and how they anticipate integrating a child into it, as well as about their network of relatives and friends.

**Daily life:** routines, such as a typical weekday or weekend, plans for childcare (if applicants work outside the home), hobbies, and interests

**Parenting:** applicants' past experiences with children (for example, their own, relatives' children, neighbors, volunteer work, babysitting, teaching, or coaching), in addition to their plans regarding discipline and other parenting issues

**Neighborhood:** descriptions of the applicants' neighborhood, including safety and proximity to community resources

**Religion/belief system:** information about the applicants' religion, level of religious practice (if applicable), and the kind of religious upbringing, if any, they plan to provide for the child

**Feelings about/readiness for adoption:** There may be a section on specific adoption issues, including why the applicants want to adopt, feelings about infertility (if this is an issue). What kind of child they might best parent? Why and how they plan to talk to their children about adoption issues. There will likely be questions about how the applicants feel about birth families and the level of openness with the birth family that would work best, depending on the type of adoption. (Note: It is very typical for families' feelings about openness to change throughout the home study process, as they learn more and become more comfortable with the issues involved.)

**Approval/recommendation:** The home study report will conclude with a summary and the social worker's recommendation. This often includes the age range and number of children for which the family is recommended.

Applicants also will be asked to provide copies of birth certificates, marriage licenses or certificates, and divorce decrees, if applicable. Some agencies share the home study with prospective parents; others do not. You may want to ask the agency about the confidentiality of the home study report and how extensively your information will be shared. Agency policies vary greatly, depending on the type of agency and type of adoption. In many cases, the information will be shared with other agencies to help unite your family with the child you are best able to parent. In some cases, information may be shared with birth parents or others.

# JUVENILE & ADULT JUSTICE

*Justice has no quantities, no colors, no shapes, and no weight—because it's an ideal, not a material substance or object.*

Source: Elizabeth S. Scott & Laurence Steinberg (Condensed for this book)

Why has the adolescent boundary between the juvenile and the adult justice systems, unbroken for 100 years, almost disappeared in less than 25 years? It is because there was an over-reaction against the extreme liberal policies of the 1960s (era of the Vietnam War protestors, and liberal Warren Supreme court) which began in the 1970s. By the 1980s, prison rates skyrocketed. As crime rates rose, politicians competed to show they would get tough on crime, whether the criminals were adults or juveniles.

Supporters of juvenile system reforms argue that they provided a clear-cut response to the sharp increase in violent youth crime that began in the late 1980s-an increase that made it painfully evident that the juvenile justice system was inadequate to the task of protecting the public from the threat of young predators. 21st century juvenile offenders are very different from the young troublemakers of fifty years ago. The juvenile court, established at the turn of the last century, was a key part of the Progressive Era's improvements.

By the early 1990s, two key premises of the rehabilitation were discredited: Young offenders were blameless, misguided children who were simply in need of redirection with the guidance of the court. This compassionate image of delinquent youths served a useful political purpose in the early twentieth century when social reformers were promoting their new court to legislatures and the public. However, it was *naive* when applied to older youths (16-18 years) committing violent crimes.

The sole purpose of state intervention in delinquency cases was to promote the welfare for youths through rehabilitative interventions. Though fervently defended by the architects of the juvenile court, this premise also was deeply flawed. It rested completely on an optimistic prediction that rehabilitation would "cure" young offenders of their criminal propensities, a prediction that allowed the Progressive Liberal reformers to avoid confronting the public's interest in protection from youth crime.

When it became clear that juvenile correctional programs were failing to reduce recidivism, the incompatible interests of the state and that of youths involved in crime became obvious. The rise in juvenile crime was seen as evidence not only that the juvenile justice system was too soft on young criminals, but also that the system's well-intentioned rehabilitative interventions were completely unsuccessful.

Disappointed youth advocates introduced far-reaching reform initiatives in the 1960-70s. These critics argued that the problem with the juvenile justice regime was not the failure of rehabilitation, but the failure of the system to deliver the proper treatments it promised while at the same time denying juveniles procedural rights provided to adult criminal defendants.

In 1967, the Supreme Court responded to this challenge in *re Gault*, a landmark opinion that extended to juveniles in delinquency proceedings some of the same constitutional rights that defendants in criminal proceedings enjoy under the Due Process Clause of the Fourteenth Amendment—most important, the right to an attorney. Gault marked, "the beginning of the end" of the traditional juvenile courts.

Decades would pass before there were serious challenges to the idea that juvenile offenders should be subject to treatment that is more lenient in the juvenile system. Gault dealt a harsh blow to the already faltering rehabilitative model. No rationale for maintaining a separate juvenile justice system emerged to replace the traditional structure. Although youths continued to be processed in the juvenile system, it was not clear what its purposes should be or how it should differ from the adult system.

Youth Violence and Law Reform as Moral Panic Advocates for tougher laws governing youth violence focused on three themes: Young offenders (typically age 15-18) were not children but dangerous criminals; violent juvenile crime was an epidemic, partly due to the laxity of juvenile court dispositions. Rehabilitation was a dismal failure, at least when it came to reforming serious juvenile offenders.

A growing chorus of angry critics argued that youth crime policy should focus primarily (or even exclusively) on the goal of protecting the public. These critics ridiculed the juvenile system for coddling youths, whom they depicted as hardened criminals who deserved "adult time for adult crime."

We argue that most adolescents should *not* be subject to the same procedures and punishment as adults, but we recognize the legitimacy of the concerns about violent youth crime that drove the reforms. The fact remains that violent crime did increase during the 1980s and early 1990s, and the epidemic spread of illegal drugs and availability of handguns made crimes more lethal and young offenders more dangerous. In the early 1990s, homicides by juveniles were at an all-time high, several times the number in 1970.

Scientific evidence confirms what parents of adolescents surely know, that although (age 13-17) teenagers are not childlike, they are less competent decision makers than are adults. Although adolescents' capacities for reasoning and understanding ("pure" cognitive abilities) approach adult levels by about age sixteen, the evidence suggests they are [far] *less capable* than adults of using these capacities in making real-world choices. *More important is that emotional and psychosocial development lags behind cognitive maturation.* For example, teenagers are considerably more susceptible to peer-to-peer influences than are adults, more likely to focus on immediate rather than long-term consequences, more impulsive and subject to mood fluctuations. They are also more likely to take risks and less skilled in balancing risks versus rewards. Finally, personality identity is fluid and unformed in adolescence. This is a period when individuals separate from their parents, experiment (often in risky endeavors), and struggle to figure out *who they really are*.

Psychological immaturity of adolescents affects decision-making and is relevant to justice policy. Immature judgment plays a role in decisions by teenagers to engage in criminal activity, and the developmental influences combine to distinguish the criminal choices of adolescents from those of adults. The differences between teenagers and adults are more subtle than those that distinguish young children (below 13) and severely impaired persons from ordinary criminals, but they are substantial and justify the conclusion that the punishment imposed on young offenders should be less severe than that which adult criminals receive. Due to their immaturity, adolescents are less capable than adult defendants in participating effectively in a court proceeding. There are constitutional restrictions on adjudicating defendants who fail to meet basic standards of trial competence.

Developmental psychologists view *adolescence as a critical stage* in an individual's development. It is a period where decision-making capacities begin to mature. It is also during adolescence that individuals begin to learn many essential skills required for optimal functioning in adulthood. The basic capacities needed to fulfill the conventional adult roles of spouse, employee, and citizen are acquired through the ordinary, hopefully healthy and "normal," experiences of adolescence.

Severe disruption of this process may impede, or completely sidetrack, the transition to productive adulthood. The successful completion of these developmental tasks involves reciprocal interactions between the adolescent and his or her social environment, an important consideration for the structuring of correctional programs. Scientific knowledge about patterns of criminal behavior in adolescence and early adulthood also plays an important role in our developmental model. Ironically, many of the developmental factors that make the criminal conduct of adolescents less culpable than that of adults also contribute to the tendency of many teenagers (especially males) to get involved in criminal activity. This tendency is so pervasive that psychologist Terrie Moffitt, one of the world's leading experts on the development of antisocial behavior, has described delinquent behavior as "a normal part of teenage life." It is not surprising, then, that *seventeen-year-olds commit more crimes than any other age group.* After that age, the crime rate declines dramatically. Predictably, as normative adolescents move into adulthood, they mature in all areas of psychological development, and, of particular importance, most of them also desist from criminal activity. A much smaller group of more intractable youths, who are described as "life-course-persistent" offenders by Moffitt, continue to engage in criminal activity beyond early adulthood. Policy should pay attention to these diverse patterns, and consider the impact of sanctions on a young offender's transition to adulthood.

The boundary between childhood and adulthood is (generally) ages 18-21, the age of majority. In this classification scheme, adults are assumed competent, autonomous persons who are responsible for their choices, while minors, whether they are toddlers or teenagers, are presumed to be incompetent, dependent, and not responsible. *There is no middle ground where most issues are concerned.* For the most part, this binary approach works quite well, although it often distorts the developmental reality of adolescence. It has not worked well, however, in juvenile justice policy.

The rehabilitative model of juvenile justice collapsed, in part, due to its naive characterization of delinquent youths as innocent children who were not responsible for their crimes. The contemporary model errs in the other direction, depicting youths who are legal minors for all other purpose as adults when it comes to criminal adjudication and punishment.

*The contemporary approach is deficient on both theoretical and practical grounds.* It offends the core principles of proportionality and due process that is deeply embedded in our criminal justice system, and is essential to its fairness. Proportionality holds that criminal punishment must be based not only on the harm of the offense, but also on the actor's blameworthiness. A justice system that is ready to hold adolescent offenders fully responsible for their crimes *violates proportionality* because young lawbreakers are less blameworthy than are their adult counterparts due to developmental immaturity.

### The Developmental Model and Principles of Criminal Law Fairness
*Consider proportionality, a bedrock principle of the criminal law.*

Proportionality seems a rather abstract concern, but it is crucial to the legitimacy of state-sponsored punishment and an important dimension of a fair and stable juvenile justice system. Indeed, some of the ridicule directed at the traditional juvenile court and the uneasy response to recent punitive reforms may reflect public concerns about accountability and fairness. Scientific research and theory support the conclusion that adolescents, even 16-17-year-olds, make decisions to get involved in criminal activity that are less culpable than those of adults, largely because their choices are driven by developmental factors that contribute to immature judgment. Adolescents are also not young children whose crimes should be excused. Thus, mitigation should apply to their criminal conduct.

The developmental model holds that adolescents are responsible for their criminal conduct and should be sanctioned for their misdeeds but deserve less punishment than do typical adult offenders. The principle of proportionality is at the heart of the substantive criminal law, but procedural fairness is also an important element of a satisfactory system for regulating youth crime. The U.S. Constitution requires that defendants in criminal proceedings be competent to stand trial, but substantial research indicates that the capacity of younger adolescents to function adequately in the trial context is highly uncertain. This evidence has important implications both for the adjudication of youths in criminal court and for formulating a competence standard in juvenile delinquency proceedings. It often seems to be the source of confusion, and should be underscored, that the issues of culpability and competence are quite distinct; the former involves the quality of the actor's decision to engage in criminal conduct, while the latter pertains to the actor's capacity for trial participation. Juvenile justice policy that is grounded-in developmental knowledge attends to the impact of immaturity in both contexts.

Supporters of the recent reforms claim that punitive policies promote public safety and therefore serve society's interests. Their calculus is distorted, however, exaggerating the threat (and thus the social costs) of youth crime and the societal benefits of adult punishment, while miscalculating or discounting an array of potential costs of punitive policies, including *recidivism costs* and economic costs that have strained budgets in many states. Unnecessary costs exist because of legislative enthusiasm for cracking down on youth crime has swept into the adult system for many nonviolent offenders who represent little threat to public safety. To be sure, tough sanctions can reduce juvenile crime. Youths who are locked-up for long periods are not on the street committing crimes. There is little evidence that long-term incarceration is effective at deterring crime or at reducing recidivism-indeed, most evidence indicates that adult imprisonment increases juvenile re-offending.

The developmental research provides essential lessons for the construction of justice policies that promote social welfare. The first lesson is that most adolescent offenders are not heading for careers in crime, unless correctional interventions push them in that direction. Legal sanctions can have a profound impact on the trajectory of young offenders' lives and affect the likelihood that they will become productive (or at least not criminal) adults. Because adolescence is a critical developmental stage during which teenagers acquire essential competencies and skills, correctional dispositions have the potential either to disrupt or to enhance social and educational development, and thus either undermine or promote prospects for gainful employment, successful family formation, engaged citizenship, and criminal involvement.

# CONVICTS & CONVERTS

Many of today's criminals lack faith in God, and they typically represent the repeat offenders. While 75% of Americans believe that Judeo-Christian faith contains "the truth," other faiths, such as Muslims, Buddhists', Hindus' and Mormons contain *some of the truth*. If one studies statistics, they will find that over two billion people *claim* to be Christians (about half are Catholics), and 1.4 billion are Muslims, worldwide. Together that is nearly half the latest global population of seven billion people.

A large number of U.S. residents are in prison, especially in California where they had the "three strikes and you're out" law. This law had seriously burdened the prison system, their families, the taxpayers (it cost an estimated $55,000-65,000 per year to house criminals) and generally all of American society. It is also a terrible waste of humanity to be mostly mentally, physically and spiritually idle in prison.

Faith-based organizations are working to reduce recidivism and to serve the imprisoned in various ways: by seeking religious conversion, by reaching out to their family members, and by promoting legal reforms. Some also offer psychosocial evaluations and various educational courses. It is also true that some convicts suddenly "find Christ" hoping they might getting out of jail sooner. *Christ was never lost!*

The number of people imprisoned in the United States has doubled in the past two decades, while the rate of serious crime has decreased significantly. A recent article in the *National Institute of Justice Journal* noted that, "This unanticipated period of declining crime may be unique in our nation's history." One may interpret the facts—rising imprisonment rates coupled with falling crime rates—as contradictory, or as a demonstration of cause and effect. Some say: *It's the economy stupid!*

Today there are two million people in our jails and prisons; that is over $100 billion cost each year, not including prison construction. The increasing rate of imprisonment for drug-related offenses is a major reason. The FBI estimates that there will be 1,250,000 arrests this year for drug-related offenses. The U.S. incarcerates seven of 1,000 residents—an extraordinary rate by international standards. European nations (on average) incarcerate less than one in 1,000. The EU does not incarcerate for non-violent crimes, such as illegal drug abuse; instead, they treat them as "social issues."

For some, that we are locking up so many criminals is good news. For others, these statistics pose questions about policy. For many in the faith community, they indicate a large population—of prisoners—in need of support and life-changing intervention. Religious organizations have been prominently involved in both these areas—with the trend in recent years being away from an effort to reform prisons and laws, and toward an emphasis on religious conversion and reform of individual prisoners.

The purpose of incarceration "is to attempt to *reform* persons, *not* to punish them vindictively." The word "penitentiary" derives from the notion of prison as a place where the imprisoned may reflect on their misdeeds and *repent* of them—i.e., *be penitent*. This dovetails with religious concepts of changing one's life through conversion. These ministries reflect a general movement in American political thought toward support for faith-based solutions to intractable social problems.

One reason that prison inmates garner little sympathy from the public is that they are, as a group, *unrepresentative* of that public—they typically don't get an opportunity to vote (felons especially can't vote). The incarcerated are usually poor, and less educated than the general population, and suffer disproportionately from a variety of social, health problems, including mental illness.

Activism aimed at reforming the prison system inevitably brings up divisive issues of race and class. By far, the population most affected by our prison system is African-Americans. *Nationally, almost one-third of black men ages 20 to 29 are in prison, on probation, or on parole.* Help and sympathy for prisoners comes largely from the religious community. The Indiana Department of Correction estimates that volunteers spent more than 92,000 hours working with inmates in the state system last year. The majority of these hours were by Christians, particularly Evangelical Christians, but there were also Catholic, Buddhist, Jewish, Islamic, and Native American volunteers who reached out to the state's prisoners.

In summary:

1. Despite falling crime rates, the prison population in the United States today is about 2 million—the highest in the nation's history, and in the entire world.
2. America's rate of incarceration, driven largely by drug-related convictions, is far higher than most industrialized nations. The effects are disproportionate higher in African-American and some Hispanic communities.
3. Advocacy programs aimed at reforming the criminal justice system were popular among congregations during the civil rights movement of the 1960s, but have now nearly disappeared.
4. Evangelical Christians dominate prison ministries. Their primary purpose is to bring prisoners to Jesus Christ. Islam has also become popular lately.

5. Religious minorities in prison feel neglected or under-served by the system.

Edited Source: Polis Center, 1200 Waterway Boulevard, Suite 100, Indianapolis, IN 46202-2157; Phone: (317) 274-2455 fax: (317) 278-1830 e-mail: polis@iupui.edu

# GUARDIAN EFFECTIVENESS

After one is formally trained, officially certified, and selected their first case, the real fun begins. The authors suggest the following fifteen "guidelines" from our five years and thirteen case experiences, which may help GALs be more effective:

1. Find an experienced GAL/PAL to "hold your hand" and help you for at least one year. Besides the coordinator, our GAL/PAL has been fantastic.

2. Get organized! Set-up your computer word processor with pre-formatted reports, such as Visitation check lists, fill-in-the-blanks Judicial Reports, among others. Format your emails with a confidential ending message, in case your private emails accidentally get to the wrong person. *It happens!*

3. Be aware that whatever you write and send by email might be subpoenaed. Reports are *not* confidential; defense lawyers, the parents, can access them.

4. Create a "colored front sheet" in your case file with all the *essential* names, addresses, directions, phones, emails, etc., for quick access.

5. Keep your very personal notes separated. Defense lawyers have *no right* to your "work product and private notes."

6. Backup everything, at least monthly. Assume that your computer will fail.

7. Some CMs see GALs as *amateurs*, because we get into a case typically *after* the Disposition hearing, when the case plan is established. Some GALs see CMs as inexperienced and uncooperative novices. *Perception is nine-tenths of reality.* You need to develop a cooperative relationship for the sake of the children. One solution is to go with the CM on your first visitation meeting with the children and caregivers, and have coffee meetings together afterward.

8. Do not get into a conflicting relationship with the CM. They provide all the referrals for children and their caregiver. Your child and parents need these services. Do not throw anyone "under the bus" at court hearings. Try to resolve issues outside the court. If that does not work, get supervisors involved.

9. If the CM or others are not cooperating on *critical* needs, send a polite message to them and their managers. If you do not get results in 48-72 hours, go higher in the management chain. *Fight for "your" children!* Request a court order from the judge through your GAL lawyer, when it becomes necessary.

10. Your first meeting with the parents or caregivers should be announced and friendly. Other meetings should be unannounced, wherever practical. Present your GAL ID and court papers appointing you to the case. Don't act like police.

11. Do not assume anything! Trust, but *always verify*. If the state did a Home Study for safety, do your own inspection; and you will be surprised.

12. Do not be alone with the children in the bedroom; keep all doors opened. Inspect the baby and children undressed for physical marks, *with the caregiver present*.

13. Get all medical and other releases signed by the parents or the caregivers.

14. Document *everything!* You must keep records on *all* persons contacted related to the case: names, places, dates, times, phone calls, messages, and observations.

15. Preparation *before* court hearings will make you more confident. If you do not get what is for the "Best Interest" for your children, tell your GAL lawyer to object (with valid reasons) and request a Court Order (arrange it in advance).

# CHALLENGES & SOLUTIONS

**Summary of Guardian ad Litem Challenges:**

1. Pre-emptive action for families does not effectively exist at this time. We need to nip child exposure to potential (probable) parental problems much, much earlier.

2. Excessively high CM turnover rates (up to 80%), has caused serious chaos. CM changes and problems unquestionably affects GAL volunteer effectiveness.

3. Edicts from DCF in Tallassee too often are "overreactions" to situations. One example that affected *everyone* was, "all children must be present at court hearings, unless excused for valid reasons." As a result, the courtroom became a zoo, and many caught child's sicknesses (including the judges). Transporting children to court was a waste of CM time and already limited resources.

4. When the central DCF computer system goes down *all* computer users statewide are down. *That's ridiculously unproductive.* A real example from a GAL supervisor: "Our computer system has been up and down all week. Try not to send me any emails today –if possible. Call if you need to tell me something urgent."

5. GALs have insufficient supervisory support; unrealistic training, sometimes lack top management support; have limited access for legal consultation; and most importantly, communication between CMs, ECA, and GALs is *very poor*.

6. CM's now provide costly referrals to the parents, frequently without sufficient follow-up. Parenting, therapies, psychological evaluations have been ineffective.

7. Children are "dumped" into *any* available foster care home, without much regard for children's age, gender, and emotional or psychological condition.

8. Many judges are *too soft*. They close parent's cases much too early. What good are all the case plans, if they are not fully followed or *incomplete*?

9. Substance abuse prevention is generally ineffective. Alcohol abuse, and illegal pills like *oxycodone*, has become a *national epidemic*. Profession help is needed.

10. Postmortem analysis of "lessons learned" from cases is rarely if ever done.

If a database containing a large enough sample of cases of injured or deceased children: by primary cause (type of injury, or cause of death), by type of caregiver responsible, by hotline source, and by action (or inaction) taken, we might learn much more about how to *prevent* similar future tragic situations.

**(See the appendix section for a summary of sample cases from Illinois).**

These observations and proposed solutions come from my professional consulting activities as a company executive. Miriam's schoolteacher experience was vitally important. She taught all age levels for 40 years, at St. Helena's High School, NYC, Greenwich High School, CT, and St. Paul's (private) Middle School, in Florida.

Our five years of GAL experiences, with thirteen cases, representing about twenty-five children, was the subject of this book. In the business world, we focus on *realistic*, no-nonsense solutions to competitive challenges. Hence, the goal of this work is to *propose positive solutions*, by thinking "outside-the-box." We are recommending practical ideas that just might help solve some of the serious *recidivism* issue for thousands of children, for incarcerated parents, for GALs and CM's who are a vital part of this system.

The number of children in the system has grown every year. It is obvious that the *root causes* are societal, cultural, spiritual, and of course, *family centered*. It will take time to change the direction towards a more positive and constructive direction.

## Problems & Solutions

GALs are usually older, and like us, many are retired. They have real-life experiences, since most had children and grandchildren of their own. Some were professionals before retiring: judges, doctors, lawyers, educators, business executives, and all volunteers deserve respect and trust by DCF, ECA and GAL management.

So what are some of the major problems with the "broken system"?

1. A few supervisors (overloaded with cases) tend to make unreasonable "demands," without considering the actual case situation, the experience (or lack of experience) and age of the individual GALs.

2. Some supervisors seem to be more concerned about CYA and PC issues, instead of diligently supporting their GALs. Some

supervisors give more credibility to parent's complaints, without asking GAL for the facts.

3. If GAL informs the supervisor of their observed situation, there is generally no need to double-check it. *Absence of trust is unacceptable.*

4. GALs are required to create JRs two weeks before the court hearing. After reviewed by the attorney and supervisor, they should send the edited document back *promptly*, not 24 hours before the judge gets a copy.

5. Supervisors should not change the content of any JR, without first getting agreement from the original GAL authors. *That is unacceptable!*

6. A 15-30 minute meeting between GALs and their attorney before court is *essential*. Otherwise, a conflict might (will) arise in front of the judge.

7. Too many different parental release forms needed to get access to medical, therapy and other essential private information for GAL investigation.

**Confidentially.** Child protection officials tend to "over-interpret" confidentiality law, believing it requires them to say nothing at all about their work, said Kendall Marlowe, executive director of the National Association of Counsel for Children and former head of caseworkers in Illinois. "There is no good reason for child welfare systems to be as secretive as they are," he said. "If the law is too restrictive, change the law."

Marlowe said he believes there is a "growing movement toward transparency." For decades, secrecy has led to finger pointing toward child welfare, but if the public were allowed to hear it, they would learn how many other systems—courts, health care, law enforcement—are involved in protecting kids, he said. "What transparency would show is that child welfare is a complex system that needs the active participation of the entire community," he said.

The media scream that children are dying, focusing on examples of child welfare workers not acting aggressively enough in taking kids from their parents, and the child welfare system, meanwhile, we can't talk about it. The field has too long hidden behind confidentiality of families. "We are spending the taxpayers' money to protect children. We owe it to the public to openly explain what we are doing to protect kids."

In the case of the four boys rescued from squalor in Denver this fall, Denver County child protection authorities said they were frustrated they could not talk about their prior involvement with the family but that they must guard the trust of families who need intervention. As for finding out whether the parents will lose rights to the boys, now in foster care, those court records are not public in this state.

"The real discussion is how we balance the privacy rights of families and children with the public's right to know if our systems are working," said Stephanie, executive director of the Rocky Mountain Children's Law Center. "This is the hard conversation that needs to take place." Source: *Jennifer Brown: jenbrown@denverpost.com*

**Budget Limitations:** During these difficult economic times, when budgets are limited, many academically qualified and experienced adults are looking for jobs. They may lack some academic courses, but they are partly qualified to be CMs. The pay will be lower than expected, but if the newly hired "associate" is willing to accept the challenge—because they have the right attitude—*an attitude of gratitude*. The associate could handle basic mundane tasks for the CM, so that they can focus on family issues.

A "balanced approach," is to have older, more experienced GALs, tag-along with younger qualified CMs, so that *both* may learn from each other. An additional benefit from this "team approach" will be better understanding and respect for each other's role in cases. Rotation of teams may also be a good idea, so that they learn from a greater variety of case situations. All managers should be required to go to the "front lines" for a few weeks or months, to see what the "real world" is really like.

"ECA is not our concern;" we were informed. "You should focus on your own issues." One high-level assistant director said, "GALs should focus on the positives. If you want to criticize and change the system, run for congress." Yet, whatever the Department of Children and Families does (or does not do) certainly affects all. *We are in these cases together*!

**Recidivism**: Criminals with long histories of serious offenses keep coming back into the system. Children of neglect and abuse grow-up and become criminals, and they in turn, come into the system. It is an *endless cycle*; with case histories that go back ten years or more. Today, nearly 31,000 children in Florida (over 550,000 nationally) are abuse or neglect cases. About 20% of those children *do not* have a Guardian ad Litem assigned to advocate for them. During the five years we have been GALs, the number of children in the system *has not declined*. As we solve current cases, old cases keep turning up.

Most (about 85-90%) of our cases have been (still are) *drug related*; i.e., parental use of addictive drugs causes domestic violence, which ultimately leads to abandonment, neglected or abused children. It is a *revolving door* of drug cases. We must face this fact: serious addicts have *limited willpower*: they will fight anyone to get their "fix." They will steal and take children's food money to buy drugs. You cannot reason with addicts; they need long-term professional help. A CDC report has confirmed this situation.

**CDC Release: Prescription painkiller overdoses at epidemic levels; kills more Americans than heroin and cocaine combined.**

The death toll from overdoses of prescription painkillers has more than tripled in the past decade, according to an analysis in the CDC Vital Signs report released today from the Centers for Disease Control and Prevention. This new finding shows that more than 40 people die every day from overdoses involving narcotic pain relievers like hydrocodone (Vicodin), methadone, Oxycodone (OxyContin), and Oxymorphone.

"Overdoses involving prescription painkillers are at epidemic levels and now kill more Americans than heroin and cocaine combined," said CDC Director Thomas Frieden, M.D., M.P.H. "States, health insurers, health care providers and individuals have critical roles to play in the national effort to stop this epidemic of overdoses while we protect patients who need prescriptions to control pain."

The increased use of prescription painkillers for nonmedical reasons (without a prescription), along with growing sales, has contributed to the large number of overdoses and deaths. In 2010, 1 in every 20 people in the United States age 12 and older—*12 million people*—reported using prescription painkillers, *non-medically* according to the National Survey on Drug Use and Health. Based on the data from the Drug Enforcement Administration, sales of these drugs to pharmacies and health care providers have increased by more than 300 percent since 1999.

"Prescription drug abuse is a *silent epidemic* that is stealing thousands of lives and tearing apart communities and families across America," said Gil Kerlikowske, Director of National Drug Control Policy. "From day one, we have been laser-focused on this crisis by taking a comprehensive public health and public safety approach. All of us have a role to play. Health care providers and patients should be educated on the risks of prescription painkillers. Parents and grandparents [should] take time to properly dispose of any unneeded or expired medications from the home and to talk to their kids about the misuse and abuse of prescription drugs."

Already, 48 states have implemented state-based monitoring programs designed to reduce diversion and doctor shopping while protecting patient privacy and the Department of Justice has conducted a series of takedowns of rogue pain clinics operating as "pill mills."

The prescription painkiller death rates among non–Hispanic whites and American Indians/Alaska Natives were *three times* those of blacks and Hispanic whites. In addition, the death rate was highest among persons aged 35–54 years. Overdose resulted in 830,652 years of potential life lost before age 65 years, a number comparable to the years of potential life lost from motor vehicle crashes and much higher than the years of potential life lost due to homicide.

For the analysis, CDC reviewed state data on fatal drug overdoses, nonmedical use of prescription painkillers, and sales of prescription painkillers to pharmacies and health care providers. The study found:

- State death rates from overdoses (from 2008 data) ranged from a *high of 27.0 deaths per 100,000 people in New Mexico* to a low of 5.5 deaths per 100,000 people in Nebraska.

- Nonmedical use of prescription painkillers ranged from a *high of 1 in 12 people aged 12 and older in Oklahoma* to a low of 1 in 30 in Nebraska. States with more nonmedical use tend to have more deaths from drug overdoses.

- Prescription painkiller sales per person were *more than three times higher in the highest state,* **Florida**, than in the lowest state, Illinois. States with higher sales per person tend to have higher death rates from drug overdose.

# PRE-EMPTIVE ACTION

If one is a witness or has evidence of abandonment, neglect or abuse of any child, they have a *moral responsibility* to call the Child Abuse Hotline or 911. After the call, the Child Protection Investigator (CPI) checks the facts about the *alleged* child neglect or abuse. If there are no visible marks on the body of the child, CPI has a difficult time proving abuse. Definitive evidence must exist before state law enforcement gets involved. If *multiple* Hotline call concerns the same family, the call records should never be deleted. Another CPI should do a more detailed investigation. Do they fit a known profile?

Today, guardians, teachers, relatives, and neighbors *cannot* take action to protect a child who is *"not in the system."* Existing law requires children to be "damaged" before action is taken. The issue is how can we save children from neglect and abuse *before* it reaches this critical stage—*before* psychological and/or physical damage actually occurs?

How does one do that? Day care staff, schoolteachers and counselors are best qualified to detect and report symptoms of possible neglect and abuse; such as bruises on the child's body; sleepy or moody kids; unresponsive children; strange behaviors; poor attendance; lack of child classroom participation; among other symptoms. School nurses or counselors should report the concerns of the teacher and have an "official" visit the home to investigate further, before it gets out-of-hand.

If the parent or caregiver ignores this early guidance then a *special* "Pre-Emptive Magistrate" should get involved, and take *corrective action*. This "early detection and intervention" capability should reduce future caseloads in the DCF dependency system—and save taxpayers millions.

**Transformation:** Florida's Department of Children and Families "transformation" policy might be a good attempt to improve their broken system. However, it does not safeguard children who are *not* in present danger, who are in *imminent danger*. The difference is between a threat that could materialize at that moment—or "present danger"—and a threat that might materialize tomorrow—or "*imminent danger.*"

The Florida example is the case of 2-year-old Ezra Raphael, beaten to death by his mother's boyfriend. He is one of *seven* Florida children who have died in 2013, despite having earlier contact with DCF. Ezra became the agency's concern because his mother had left him with a woman she scarcely knew. DCF goes to the woman's home and finds Ezra *right now* is in a good place. However, if the child returned to his mother, he would be in *imminent danger*. DCF makes a note in the file to "call us if mom tries to come and pick up the child," and *they closed the investigation*."

The mother came for Ezra in April, and he died in June. His former caregiver said she tried to keep the child, but the agency told her *"there was nothing that they could do. ... They had closed the case,"* she said.

DCF had one encounter with Ezra in February 2013. At that time, Ezra was in the care of a non-relative caregiver. "The caregiver did not have legal guardianship or custody of the child. However, the child was "determined to be safe," according to DCF. That's one of the chief problems, because under the [new] rule, DCF wouldn't be required to develop a safety plan for Ezra. "Under the transformation framework, [only] *present danger* requires a safety plan or removal. **Imminent danger does not require action, and that exposes children to serious risk of harm.**

**Dependency Law:** Judges *do not* (should not) make laws. They *do not* focus on what the law *ought* to be. They enforce existing laws—they interpret what the law says. Dependency law is relatively new: it is limited, it is questionable; it is an advocacy system. Judges and defense lawyers for parents are not primarily there for the "**best interest**" of the child. They are interpreters of law; they don't focus on the child.

**Court-appointed Attorneys:** If parent's claim to be needy, they sign an "Affidavit of Insolvency," and naturally they get free legal services. Repeat offenders of child neglect and abuse get *everything* from the state (taxpayers), without paying a dime. Examples of free services provided to defendant(s): referrals for services, such as: psychologists, psychiatrists, various therapies, drug abuse treatments, couples counseling, anger management or domestic violence classes, food stamps, housing allowances, etc., etc. The defendant duly sworn says, *"I do not have enough income to hire a lawyer. Any property I own is of little value and I cannot sell to hire a lawyer* (legally sworn statements)."

In many cases parents have sufficient income, they own a home, and have hidden bank accounts or trust funds. With tens-of-thousands of defendant cases each year, a very high percentage of them *falsely* claim to be "needy." In contrast, middle-class, mostly white defendants, with limited assets, are required to pay thousands of dollars for these same services, and if they lose the case, they pay court costs as well. Repeat offenders *are experts*; they know extremely well how to "milk this court dependency system." Conclusion: "allegedly poor" repeat offenders have more rights than others.

**New Born Protection:** Parents currently in the state system because of child neglect or abuse, related to drug issues, domestic violence, who are doing their case plan, might have another child during this same timeframe. The newborn child is *not protected* under the current case plan. The legal theory: "Parents have a right to procreate, and until one can prove neglect or abuse, the state should not interfere." We agree with this *theoretically,* but the law should deal with many exceptions that we have encountered in our cases. Drug addicted persons are "rabbits" that reproduce constantly, producing drug addicted "little bunnies" for the state and hospitals to care for. *That is crazy!*

Example: Mary Jane and John Doe have two children and she and her paramour are in the court system because of selling illegal drugs, domestic violence, as well as a history of other issues. Both agreed to accept their case plan tasks, but he is *not* actively working on his case plan. His excuse: "I was in jail and couldn't do most of my tasks." After released from jail, his drug habits and violence problems continue. They represent an *imminent danger* to their children, as reported during GAL visitations, and at the Judicial Review. However, the state and the CM tell the Magistrate: "the parent's case plan tasks has really improved; they are making excellent progress."

The magistrate asks GAL "is there is *actual safety issues* with the parents and children?"

GAL answers honestly: "We have no factual evidence, but there is '*imminent danger*' because they have not completed *all* of their case tasks and they were serious addicts."

The magistrate overrules our objections, and orders reunification of the children with their parents within 30 days. A few weeks later, the *delayed* urine analysis arrives for the parents. Results show *positive cocaine* usage. Our *instincts* were right (however, we cannot depend on instincts without evidence). The State and CM call for and urgent hearing. The Magistrate cancels her reunification order, *just in time.*

# MOTIVATIONS & INCENTIVES

What are the motives and incentives for CMs, the State, and the Judge? Is it to close as many cases as possible, and save the state money? Absolutely! What are the defense lawyer's motives and incentives? It is to get the parent(s) cleared. Yes, they certainly do not fight to save the parent's children—*it is not their role*. What are *Guardian ad Litem* motives and incentives? Our *one and only goal* is to be strong independent advocates (voices) for the **Best Interest of the Children.**

**Volunteerism:** My spouse encouraged me to volunteer at the local St. Vincent de Paul soup kitchen. After learning that it was *truly* a charitable operation, feeding 200-250 poor and homeless, *every day*, I agreed to get involved. After courses in cooking, I became responsible for Monday meals. It was a rewarding experience serving the poor and homeless. We had a prayer before each meal, until the government terminated it.

One day I learned that *some* of the local police were harassing the homeless. After taking a simple survey to learn exactly what was going on, and gather evidence, I learned that police officers were beating the homeless and tearing up poor people's I.D. cards, so that they would have difficulty cashing Social Security checks. I complained to the director. She told me, *"They must be doing something wrong."*

My request to correct this situation fell on deft ears. *"I trust the police,"* she said. Unknown to me was the little detail that the police chief was on the board of directors. I went to the press with my story. Since the press article embarrassed the police chief, I lost from my first good volunteer job. (One has to move on to other works of charity).

Therefore, we believe that government *must* provide a "safety net" for those who are truly poor, sick or disadvantaged. Nevertheless, the "War on Poverty" by LBJ was a complete failure and waste of money. Things have gone to extremes from 2009 to 2013:

- Disability payments climbed from $115 to $139 billion;
- Food stamps went from $54 to $80 billion annually.
- Welfare grew from $162 to $196 billion; and
- Medicaid has rocketed to $55.6 billion.
- Unemployment remains at 6.5 % ("real" unemployment is about 12.6%).
- Poverty has increased, especially among African-Americans and Hispanics. Nearly 25% of all young adults, ages 18-25, are now living with their parents.

***The problem with socialism is that other people's money runs out.***
***—Margaret Thatcher***

Our "progressive" government programs have created a *disincentive* for people to work. There have been advantaged and disadvantaged in *all* societies, from the beginning of recorded history. Today a large majority of "good doers" wish to lay claim upon, or monopolize minorities, or those who are disadvantaged. Scandalous judicial decisions are made on a regular basis, based on claims of "disadvantaged minorities."

A person's attitude and state of mind (a fully formed conscience, a sense of right and wrong) determines one's fate in life. You become what you "think" you will "become." If you think' you can, you can. If you think you can't, you can't. In either case, you are right. If anyone feels disadvantaged, try to define why you think it is so. Then do what you need to do to correct your situation, lawfully. No one else has the most to gain. No one else has the motivation required to improve your situation. Just thinking about it is not going to make it happen. Do you have this motivation? Only your effort and action, and determined passion will make it happen!

1. **CM and GAL Conflicts.** We frequently get into unnecessary adversary situations, fighting over various child and parental case plan issues.

   **Solution:** Cooperation and mutual support can and should be encouraged by management between the parties, while maintaining independence, as required. Instead of CMs making two monthly-required visits to the children and caregivers, one trip could be made by the GAL, and then they can get together to share notes and suggest follow-up action, if required. GALs are required to make one visit per month, anyway. Sharing visitation info would save both significant time and money. Both parties could also share PAR results and therapy info, thus saving duplication of effort. Monthly meetings between GAL and CM, comparing progress would be a great idea.

2. **Caregivers vs. Child Needs.** Children, who do *not* require special or medical foster care, are "dumped" *wherever* space is available. The result can be (often is) a "poor match" between the foster caregiver and the children. This is both a behavioral issue and awareness problem. By behavior, we mean that the foster mom and dad may not be aware of, or able to cope with the children's *special* emotional or mental challenges (e.g., Baker Acted kids). Typically, foster caregivers lack the history on the children. Obviously, this represents a very difficult situation for both them and children.

   By awareness issue, we mean that the children may move from a very poor home and environment, to a richer home and environment (the reverse situation may exist). What is wrong with that, one might ask? This dilemma arises when the children are reunited, and returned to their biological parents. They see a *stark contrast* between the two home environments, which can be a real shock particularly for older children. This is *especially true* when "bonding" is not established between the biological parents and children. If the child goes from a physically richer home environment into a poor foster care home, they experience similar "environmental shock."

**Solution:** It is important that "real bonding" (spontaneous love and sincere warm affection) be *confirmed* by the CM and GAL before reunification takes place. It is too easy to report to the judge that mom and dad have been "Fully Compliant" in terms of case plan "check lists" of tasks, and leave out "real bonding." One cannot generally observe *bonding* in a "fish bowl." When people are observing parents with their children, they directly affect what they observe. Parents will "act" as if they are bonding to pass the test.

One solution is to have a hidden camera in the supervised meeting room. Then one can observe them in a more natural situation. In addition, CM and GAL should *not* give children too many gifts (especially during Christmas), because it becomes a kind of "bribe" for their affection. They will also become materialistic and expect more gifts from their biological parents afterwards, and they may not be able to afford it. Teaching charity, by giving to others, should be encouraged. Children could give away their past Christmas and birthday gifts to other poor kids, before GALs give them new gifts.

Moreover, ECA and the CM should carefully try to match the foster care children with the sex, age and particular requirements of the other kids staying at the foster home. Otherwise, there can be incompatibility and chaos. It is a difficult challenge, but with the use of *modified* "computer date matching software," a better match is possible.

3. **Referral Services.** Too often the excuse given by parents for *not* doing their case plan tasks is that they were incarcerated, and therefore didn't have access to CM referral services, such as parenting courses, psycho-social evaluations, drug abuse tests, domestic violence courses, anger management, among other possible required case tasks to complete their case plans. The Judge is *required* to consider this as a possible "valid excuse," if the mom or dad are in jail during most of the case plan period under consideration.

Why did they continue to commit crimes we might ask? Why should the court decision be delayed or go in their favor, because of "*parental rights*"? Many of these child abusers know how to beat the justice system, with help from taxpayer provided court appointed defense attorneys. Again, the judge needs to follow existing laws.

**Solution:** If one cannot bring prisoners to the case plan specialist, bring the specialists to the prisoner (in non-violent cases). The answer given at a recent meeting with a judge and primary services management was it is more expensive. "Whose budget would be willing to bare this extra expense?" They asked. This seemed to be a showstopper.

What if prison guards, who have the basic budget to transport prisoners to/from jails to court proceedings on a daily basis, *also* transport them to preplanned referral meetings. *We solved the budget problem!* The guards have the people resources, transportation vehicles, and security assets to perform these extra tasks, with a relatively minor increase in budgets. This extra set of vital tasks might make their jobs more interesting, more meaningful and certainly more productive. Why not try it as a "test case?" The solution to case plan task referral scheduling: *Do it more wisely*!

4. **Parenting Courses.** Based on direct observations with cases, it is clear that many parents still do not know much about real-life parenting, *after* they received "certificates of completion." Either

they were sleeping during class, or the course is ineffective? These required classes should not just deal with the basics of parenting.

**Solution:** Parenting classes should also be case-specific, whenever possible; it should *not* only be about generalized parenting. It should include case-specific topics and role- playing, where parents are paired-off, and each parent member of a case-specific team, plays the reverse role, and thus sees the viewpoint from their children's perspective.

5. **Problem Addiction.** We clearly have an extremely serious drug addiction problem, *nationwide*. About 80-85% of our cases start with addiction. In an article published on July 16, 2010, ABC News reported that pain medicine addiction had risen "400 percent in the last decade." Although that statistic is frightening enough, it does nothing to describe the horror this demon wields on a family when it strikes home personally.

Parents of a prescription drug addict can attest that life as they used to know stopped when their daughter or son were injured in any major accident. After consulting with injury lawyers, and after going to chiropractors and a "pain management clinics," hell on earth usually begins. As his/her abuse of OxyContin [among other addictive drugs] grows, their ability to invent extremely intricate lies grows as well.

What many people may not know is how powerfully addicting medications, such as *OxyContin, oxycodone, hydrocodone*, and their acetaminophen-combined partners such as *Percocet* and *Roxicet* can be when they abuse pain medications. Many people were initially introduced to opiates from valid prescriptions due to pain from injuries. As tolerance of the drug increased, the desire to take more increased. Depression, nervousness, insomnia, and low or high blood pressure are reported as some of the adverse reactions associated with discontinuance of opiates.

Opiates are very expensive! So how does an addict afford to keep his habit going? He or she lies, cheats, steals, and may pawn their parent's property, or anyone else's that they can get their hands on, such as milk and food money for their children. Then they get hold of the next script and sell each pill at approximately $10 and $25. They can easily earn $2,000-5,000 per week. Its illegal drug trafficking. What is the alternative?

Each time one has been arrested, however, (all of these incarcerations are typically for non-violent offenses) they avowed that they have learned their lesson and will *never* touch this "demon" again. They also want to find a good job. They want to finish college education. Realistically, no one wants to hire a "criminal felon," and so the new demons related with rejection, depression, and low self-esteem crops up.

**Solution:** Teens in high school, *with parental or caregiver approval*, should be *required* to take monthly random urine analysis for drugs. The results must be confidential, and directly reported to the primary caregiver or parent. If the teen refuses the test, then they are "probable suspects," for drug usage. That should be reported to the legal caregiver (not to police or law officials). The school nurse and security personnel must supervise random UAs. If this plan can save thousands of young lives, and reduce addiction treatment costs, it just might be worth trying it.

6. **Grandparents as Caregivers.** ECA should *not* consider older relatives (65 or older), *especially* sick senior grandparents as caregivers for their grandchildren. They usually become incapacitated or die, leaving the children with another traumatic move to some other stranger family or caregiver. This does not make sense; it is *dumb*, and in the end, it is more expensive, not to speak of the terrible emotional shock on the children.

We had this happen in one of our cases, where the children had to move three times, in a few months, before adopted, after the TPR trial and Appeal. The children really suffered during this *unnecessary* switching of caregivers. It is *false economics* for the state to use this type of older, sick relative caregivers to save money.

**Solution:** We must *first* consider the impact on the children. It is far better for a child to have fewer moves, with only one final move to permanency, in the adoption process. Budget limits should *NOT* be the major determining factor for the placement of kids.

7. **Insufficient GAL Volunteers.**

   **Solution:** Greater state funding, including marketing to make people more aware of the Guardian ad Litem program works of charity. In addition, provide compensation for GAL transporting cost based on logs kept for all case related work.

**Root Causes of Family Problems:**

1. **Parental Guidance:** If the parents are dysfunctional, chances are the children will follow the same pattern, unless someone steps in and helps them before they grow-up, and also become *dysfunctional parents.*

2. **Faith in God:** If there is no "moral compass," most will be lost. We are all persons with souls, therefore, *spiritual beings.*

3. **Rebelling:** If parents and teachers are too strict, their children often rebel. Lighten-up on sternness—*but, not too much.*

4. **Role Models:** When parents, teachers, movie actors, and government officials are not ethical, or say one thing, and then do another, *children emulated them.*

5. **Friends:** Peer pressure is a powerful force that our youth follow. Teach them to seek out good, *real friendships*.

6. **Addiction**: Addiction causes loss of free will, *the inability to function mentally*.

7. **Independence**: As long as your children are under *your roof*, they have no "private" bedrooms; you have a right to control whatever they do in your home.

8. **Criminal Activities**: Often leads to incarceration, which leads to further acts of crime. Society must take proactive action early to *nip it before it buds*.

9. **Family Support**: Family members may be better equipped at rescuing troubled youth, and professionals or faith-based helpers could (should) step in and aid troubled young parents and their children.

While this book focused on many of the challenges of our society and culture, the authors want to leave the reader with some **"*positive ideas*."**

## Psychology

Herbert Benson, in his publication *Timeless Healing*, exposed Freud's views of religion as "entirely fallacious." In *The Future of Illusion* (1927), Sigmund Freud, one of the *extreme atheists* of the 20th century, concluded that faith is a form of "mental disorder," a "universal obsession neurosis," rooted in "infantile" and "narcissistic" patterns of thought.

"No nation outside of Germany and Austria was more hospitable to psychoanalysis than America," notes Mark Edmundson in "*The Death of Freud*." Freud understood that we would embrace his theories. "We are bringing them the plague," he told colleagues when disembarking in New York. And they don't even know it."

Freud's claimed success for treatments that actually failed, such as the famous "Dora" and "Horace Frink" cases. In the judgment of psychiatrist Peter D. Kramer, writing in *"Freud: Inventor of the Modern Mind,"* Freud "was more devious and less original than he made himself out to be, and where he pioneered, he was often wrong. Freud displayed bad character in the service of bad science."

A recent Harris poll found that nearly one in three American adults had "received treatment or therapy from a psychologist or other mental health professionals."

Freud predicted that strait-laced Americans would never embrace his ideas "once they discover the sexual core of our psychological theories." Of course, in America sex sells. It is probably one of the biggest reasons that Freud's theories gained such currency here. As so much else, he was wrong about that, too. Source: summarized from: *"One Hundred Years of Freud in America."* See Wall Street Journal, August 7, 2009

## Faith Heals

Ironically, recent scientific research has shown that, far from being a neurosis or source of such, religious belief is one of the "most consistent correlates of overall mental health and happiness." Study after study shows a powerful relationship between religious belief and practice, and healthy behaviors in many vital areas as:

1. Reducing suicide rates (Kubler-Ross, *On Children and Death*, Collier, 1983).
2. Lowering drug abuse (Melvin Morse, *Closer to the Light*, Ivy Books, 1990).
3. Declines in divorce rates (Fenwick, *The Truth in the Light*, Berkley, 1995).
4. Curtailing depression ((Melvin Morse, *Closer to the Light*, Ivy Books, 1990).

These authors certainly do not propose that society eliminate psychotherapeutic treatment, especially where other therapies have failed. However, much of the empirical data runs *contrary* to the earlier consensus of the psychotherapeutic profession. For example, David B. Larson, former National Institutes of Health psychiatrist, writes in "*Have Faith: Religion Can Heal Mental Ill's*":

If a new health treatment was discovered that helped to reduce the rate of teenage suicide, prevent drug and alcohol abuse, improve treatment for depression, reduce recovery time from surgery, lower divorce rates and enhance a sense of well-being, one would think that every physician in the world would be scrambling to try it. Yet, what if critics denounced this treatment as harmful, despite research findings that showed it to be effective more than 80% of the time? Which would you be more ready to believe—the assertions of critics based on *opinions*, or the results of the clinical trials based on solid statistical data and research?

The "new health treatment" Larson is talking about is "Christian religious faith."

## American Constitution

Many of today's political leaders would not have signed the Declaration of Independence because it contains words they cannot accept, such as: "Creator," "Truth," and "Equality." Pending changes in Supreme Court Judges *may* finally shift it away from the extreme liberal recent past, toward a more conservative and traditional decisions in the future. However, it has not happened yet. Hopefully that will mean that earlier irrational rulings on "individual rights" may soon be reversed, especially abortion-on-demand, forbidding of school prayer, allowing gay marriages, permitting the burning of the American Flag, forbidding Christmas and Jewish symbols in public places, and the approval of the "right" to allow old or terminally ill patients to have a so-called "happy death." As these laws are changed, this country may once again become, "*One Nation under God*."

## Education

> *If you think education is expensive, try ignorance.*
> —Derek Bok

> *Give a man a fish and you feed him for a day;*
> *teach a man to fish and you feed him for a lifetime.*

The public education system clearly needs a major overhaul; and it will never happen unless forced to change. Everyone seems to cry for "free choice"—"woman's choice," "sexual choice," among other choices. Why not "school choice." Clearly, the current public school system, where costs per student have actually doubled on average in the last decade, while student performance results have remained flat, does not work. Many states have now passed laws allowing student vouches for private schools. Democracy cannot function without an educated and well-informed society. Democracy depends on an educated population.

During National School Choice Week, an opportunity arises to celebrate educational choice in all forms and the positive impact choice has had on so many children. Throughout this week, tens-of-thousands of kids who have benefited from a variety of choice programs attend rallies all over America. These children are fighting for more educational choice options including private and religious schools, opportunity scholarships, charter schools, and public school choice. Unfortunately, far too many adults are on the sidelines while our children are standing up to the *educational status quo*. As history has shown, children are one of the best advocates for real change.

Democracy *cannot* function in a poorly educated and ill-informed society. While many of the demonic expressions of Atheistic-Humanism were defeated in World War II and the Cold War, lots of 'intellectual and moral toxins' still remain. For example, many less educated Moslem masses in Palestine elected terrorist leaders to run the country in 2006. Lebanon Muslims voted for Hezbollah (terrorist group) to be part of that government. What is the result so far? It is chaos for most of them!

Europe and the Americas are not immune from these *poison toxins* of socialism and dictatorships. Consider some of the characters that were actually elected to high office in Russia (ex-KBG Chief, Putin), Spain (an extreme Socialist), Venezuela (Chavez, a Communist).

> *If we wish to bring about a more compassionate—and therefore a fairer society—it is essential that we educate our children to be responsible, caring human beings. The human mind is both the source, and properly directed, the solution to all our problems. ...*
> —The Dalai Lama

Education is much more than a matter of imparting the knowledge and skills by which narrow goals are achieved. It is also about opening the child's eyes to the needs and rights of others. The preamble to the *Declaration of Independence* referred to 'Nature and Natures' God, and ends 'with a firm reliance on the protection of Divine Providence.' God is in our Constitution, and the Congress begins each day with a prayer. The U.S. dollar says, 'In God We Trust.' Yet, our public education system, which began as Christian schools, has become secular if not anti-Christian, where group prayers are no longer permitted.

## Universities

Our Universities have become a solid bastion of *extremely* liberal viewpoints, as demonstrated by two articles in a recent issue of the scholarly journal Current Reviews. One article presents a survey of academic social scientists, which I will not review here, because it is not simply about Republican versus Democratic teachers and scholars; it is about *attitudes*. A second article studied voter registration of California college professors and found that the ratio of registered Democrats to Republicans is 5 to 1, with sociology departments showing a ratio of 44 Democrats to 1 Republican, but economics departments employing 2.8 Democrats for each member of the GOP.

*St. Petersburg Times* (Aug. 5, 2006) *Academia's Stultifying Swamps* by Debra J. Saunders

"While liberal professors often think that they are open-minded, Daniel B. Klein of George Mason University believes that they also often think that 'we're smarter' than those outside of academia, which gives them a right to 'discriminate against people who get it wrong.' In their 'groupthink,' many social scientists marginalize heterodox thinkers," Saunders suggests. "As a result, many conservative professors might be afraid to share their points of view, which may cause colleagues to turn on them."

The general aim of education is to train the *whole person*—the intellect and the will, not merely the mind alone. Knowledge is about the intellect; character is about the will, what decisions we make. The purpose of education is to give the mind truth—truth about *everything*: sciences, literature, history, the arts, philosophy, etc. Foremost, it is about **your purpose**; knowing why you are here, and where you plan to go. What is the primary knowledge education should give us: *What is the truth about humanity?*

America's public education system has to have serious competition from the private sector, before it will change, says Miriam, who recently retired after 40 plus years of educating our youth in both public and private schools, at all levels. "*We need to reward good teachers and rid the system of apathetic and biased teachers,*" she says.

## Family

We must respect the basic family unit, which has endured for over 3,500 years. If the family decreases who will produce future children? Europe and Russia have already encountered this problem; the fertility rate has declined to 1.8-2.0%. Where will the next generation of youth come from?

## Parenting

Parents must take responsibility for parenting. We should not depend on impersonal babysitting or childcare services, and expect these youngsters to magically grow up, and become compassionate selfless adults. (However, some of these services are exceptional). Mothers must take a few years leave from their jobs, if they expect to be "real mothers." "We cannot afford to do that," many will argue. While we must admit that is true in *some* cases, especially during difficult economic times, we would argue: *you cannot afford to do otherwise*. Which is more important, earning more money to buy *non-essential* things, and "keeping up with the Jones'," or taking care of your God-given gift, your precious living children?

Why do you have children if this is not your number one priority? Latchkey children yearn for the love they may never get! All children are born innocent. It is the parents, the education system, the role models, and the environment that causes them to become problematic. In the final analysis, the solution for many of our future social challenges, are these three fundamental factors: Faith, Family, and Education.

## Listening

People have simply stopped listening to each other. None of us really listen enough, do we? Some of us, especially today's youth too often attempt to finish your thoughts for you, because they are impatient. That's called "intellectual arrogance." The only way to know God, and to know each other, is to listen. Listening is reaching out into that other self, getting through your walls and theirs. Listening is the beginning of understanding and comprehension, and *the first exercise of true love*. The only way to find the truth is to listen with total openness, without any preconceptions.

"When I ask you to listen to me, and you start to give me advice, you have not done what I asked. When I ask you to listen to me, and you begin to tell me why I should not feel that way, you are trampling on my feelings. When I ask you to listen to me, and you feel you have to do something to solve my problems, you have failed me, as strange as that may seem. ...So please listen and just hear me. And, if you want to talk, wait a minute for your turn—and I will listen to you."

## Equality

None of us are born "equal" in any pragmatic sense of that ideal. We don't choose our parents, race, country, environment, economic situation, and most don't choose their religion. Parental nurturing must exist at an early stage. Children should be required to earn what they want (not basic needs). Adults have many civil rights, but they must demonstrate that they are "mature adults," and by this we mean, they must take responsibility for their actions. Education and religious book teaching, without real life supporting experiences and good role models, *is meaningless.*

> *If the world has lost its respect for authority, it is only because it lost first in the home. The progress and fall of civilizations depend on the moral ordering of human life. Peace is the tranquility of order, and order implies justice to God and neighbor. Peace fails when each man seeks his own and forgets the love of God and neighbor.*
> —Fulton J. Sheen

**In summary**, the five most important principles that will determine how we deal with our children's future life on planet Earth, *and Eternal Life* hereafter, includes:

1. **Parenting:** At least one loving parent is essential to guide children and to teach basic morals, manners, faith, and a sense of individual responsibility.

2. **Attitudes:** Children develop early positive or negative attitudes and behaviors, depending on the family, the school situation, the neighborhood and role models.

3. **Education:** A well-rounded education is essential. BA or BS students will earn about 3.5-4.5 times as much as most persons with only a high-school diploma. Some of our youth are not college ready. They should then have an opportunity to learn a trade. On the other hand, a good, balanced education is much more than just earnings. *Education is the key to happiness!*

4. **Role Models:** It is the duty of parents to control whomever the child hangs out with, especially after school, within the neighborhood. Parents must also control what is watched on TV and on the computer networks.

5. **Faith:** *Unless you become as little children, you shall not enter the Kingdom of Heaven* (MT 18:3). Christianity began with the worship of a babe. Without trust in God, your children and you will wander aimlessly throughout life. Without any true purpose, you and they will be lost! Remember that life here on Earth is a mere "blimp" on the total time horizon compared to Eternal life with your Creator.

## Program Funding

Source: Jan Pudlow, Senior Editor, *Florida Bar News*. (Partly edited for this book)

When Alan Abramowitz made his budget request at the [Florida] Legislature, he brought a cardboard cutout of a child to keep the focus where it belongs. "*It's a human rights issue that children be treated with dignity and that their voices are heard,*" said Abramowitz, executive director of the Florida *Guardian ad Litem* Program. He's asking for $3.9 million [additional] in FY to hire 64 additional staff positions needed to fully support the work of an additional 1,650 volunteers to provide "**best interest**" advocacy for 3,367 more children in dependency court—from the current 21,497 to 24,864. ...

Today, the GAL Program represents about 70 percent of all abused, abandoned, and neglected children in Florida's dependency system. Is 70 percent good enough? Florida Statute §39.822 would answer "no." However, the GAL Program has never truly fulfilled the statutory mandate to provide a GAL for every child. Abramowitz is just hoping to nudge back up from 70 percent to the previously reached level of 80 percent with his request to build capacity and enhance training to support more volunteers. He said he's trying to run the office as efficiently as possible, so that funds go to support more volunteers in the field. ...

His five-year plan is to represent 100 percent of Florida's abused and neglected children. Now, he is forced to triage cases to protect the most vulnerable children. "Our staff struggles every day when trying to decide whose case we can advocate for and whose case we cannot," Abramowitz said. "It's a heart-wrenching decision when we know all children deserve a GAL. We really struggle with it. It's hard to tell a child they aren't going to get a volunteer to help them." He's hopeful the day will come when the triage process is obsolete." He is heartened by support expressed by Gov. Rick Scott and legislative leaders. "I don't know of any legislator who is not supportive," Abramowitz said. "I feel I have an obligation to meet the intentions of the legislation. It requires us to provide 100 percent representation. My intention and long-term position is to strive to get there. The good thing is it's such a positive, effective program."...

Abramowitz shares an email written by Kemp Brinson, GAL volunteer of the year for the 10th Circuit in Polk County: "A few years ago, I met someone who changed my life forever. I can't tell you her name. I can't tell you what happened to put her where she was. All I can tell you is that when I read about her story for the first time, I cried. She was 13, and she slumped into the chair to my right and gave me the teenage look that says, *'I care about nothing.'* The setting was a modest foster home in rural Polk County."

Brinson chronicles how they learned to trust each other, how he tracked down her mother through a former landlord, and found her brother and father through his probation officer. "Her mother was on the verge of permanently losing parental rights. Despite all odds, when given one last chance, her mother got a job and began putting things back together. I helped dozens of other people involved understand how the system was working for her, and how it wasn't. With the help of a particularly conscientious caseworker, we were able to begin reuniting the family, little by little.

There was still a lot of pain. She had trouble with school, family, boys, and emotional issues. We talked about all these. I met some of her teachers. She even let me go to a couple of her school functions. Despite her pain and the walls erected, her intelligence, grace, and strength glimmered through. As her family situation improved, she began to shine. It was inspiring. "Eventually, the family was reunited and the case was closed. Brinson has never forgotten the child he helped give a voice in court—and her family.

"The state of Florida cannot raise children. Only people can," Brinson wrote. "I hope this amazing young woman and her siblings learned as much about life from me as I did from them. This connection happened because I fought back my apprehensions and concerns long enough to make that initial call to volunteer for the Guardian ad Litem Program. When people speak of making a difference, of living life to its fullest, this is what they mean."

Florida House Justice Appropriations
Source: GAL Executive Director (partly edited for this book)

The Guardian ad Litem Program Executive Director also makes a presentation to the House Justice Appropriations Subcommittee, every few years on what the Guardian Program would look like, or *how it will exist with a 10% cut in budget*. All agencies have to go through this exercise.

The Director explains how the Guardian Program is appointed to a child, and discusses the fact that there are currently about 32,000 children in the dependency system in Florida, and about 10,000 of those children do not have Program Services, and they do not have volunteers to advocate for them. She explains the impact of not having an independent voice in the courts, and makes it very clear that a cut of 10% would be *devastating* for children and it would require the volunteers to discharge off about 1,458 children. As the year continued, we would not be able to be the "voice" for more and more children. She explains the role of the Guardian ad Litem staff who certifies, background screens, interviews, trains and supports volunteers.

She explains how Judges rely on our "independent voices" and children have better outcomes when they have a Guardian ad Litem giving them "a voice in court system."

The Chair of the Subcommittee was very complimentary of the volunteers and the Program and told an emotional story. The Subcommittee supports our Program. At the end of her presentation, she reiterated the findings of the "Blue Ribbon Panel on Child Protection," which determined that, "*if there is any program that costs the least, and benefits the most, this is the one.*"

The Director concluded by stating that although we presented the 10% budget cut exercise, that the Guardian ad Litem was, in fact, seeking to increase our budget by 3.9 million dollars so we can increase representation of children to 80%. Although we did not lose any funds last year in the legislature, since 2007 the Guardian ad Litem, has been cut by 11% and lost 71 critical positions. Thanks to all the volunteers and staff, your commitment to children is priceless and the stories many of you have shared with me are truly inspiring. It does inspire me! The Director will continue to fight so that every child has a voice.

## Support for GALs

How can we sustain Guardians and CASA so that they may be more effective? By providing more support from the state and federal government in the following areas:

1. Additional critical people resources;
2. Better management support systems;
3. More realistic and on-going training programs;
4. Quality professional referral services (with follow up);
5. Improved communication between all groups (especially GALs and CMs);
6. Update State Statutes §39.822; and most importantly,
7. Allow *optional* faith-based support services.

# EPILOGUE

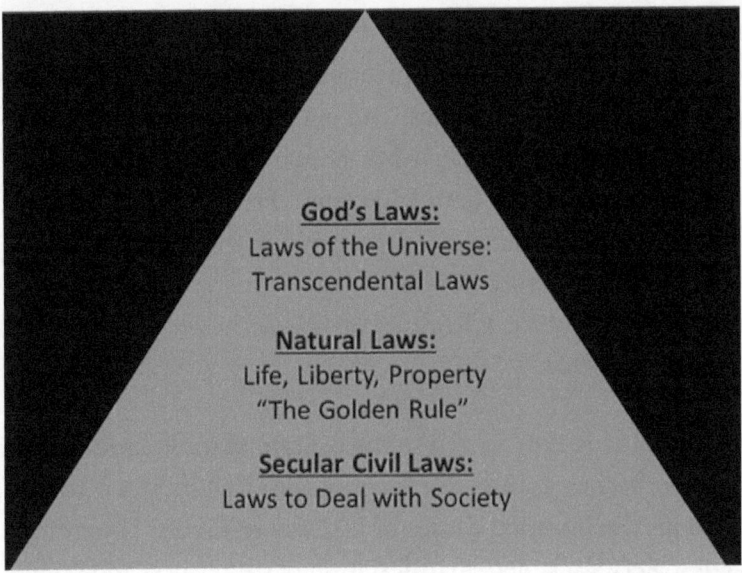

What kind of society and parents have we created? In recent decades, we have produced a "bumper crop" of dysfunctional parents and their families. They are not even good enough parents; *they are the worst parents in recent history*. Why is this so?

One might argue that our times are not unlike what existed when Nero was Emperor of the Roman Empire, 2000 years ago. Back then it was a time of widespread moral corruption, sexual permissiveness and cruelty; the worshiping of pagan gods and various occults; and the exploitation of the weaker, poorer masses of people. While this comparison may be argumentative, our children and grandchildren will encounter far greater challenges in the 21st century than humanity has ever experienced in its recent past. Why is this so? Because of lack of contentment—*basically it's greed*—that sows the seeds of envy, and aggressive competitiveness, and this in turn, leads to a society of materialism, and a general lack of compassion for others. This condition ultimately results in a widespread decline in spirituality.

## Death of the Soviet Empire

By the late 20th century, the cold war ended. The former USSR, branded as the "Evil Empire," collapsed. What replaced it? Former dictatorships, western colonies and eastern communist countries gained independence. People who gained independence, what did they do with their newly found freedom? Freedom without a rudder for the ship of state, without real purpose, without proper education, without individual responsibility, without true spirituality, produces fundamental discontent. Clearly, that is exactly what we have today: *deep-rooted discontent.*

Interestingly, in his 1987 speech to the Plenum of the Communist Party, Mikhail Gorbachev, former President of the "Evil Empire," the USSR, talked about the immoral causes of his society's crisis: "Interest in the affairs of society slackened, manifestation of callousness and skepticism appeared and the role of moral incentives to work declined. The stratum of people, some of them young people, whose ultimate goal in life was *material well-being* and gain by any means, grew wider. Their cynical stand was acquiring more and more aggressive forms, poisoning the mentality of those around them. ... An atmosphere of permissiveness was taking shape, exactingness, discipline and responsibility were declining (For further in depth coverage, see *Revolutions in Eastern Europe* by Niels Nielsen (Maryknoll, 1991), and the *Death of the Soviet Empire* by David Pryce-Jones (Holt, 1995).

After the peaceful Revolution of 1989 (predicted at Fatima, in 1917), the Soviet Union was no more by 1991. This left a cultural, moral, economic and political vacuum. As the Cold War ended, Western Europe also began to slowly slide into moral decay. With the de-Christianization of society, Europe became infected by this atheistic- humanism disease, especially more socialistic France, Germany, and Belgium. (The EU did not even acknowledge *any contribution of Christianity* in their new constitution).Whom do you think is next? Earlier Empires that rose and fell, in our 3,500-year of recorded history, include Egyptian, Babylonian, Persian, Greek, Roman, Ottoman, Spanish, British, German, and Russian (USSR). Most declined from lack of leadership and *corruption from within*. Again, who do you think is the next to go?

America is becoming socialistic (distribution of wealth by government *without* voter approval), focuses on excessive political correctness (PC), has an absence of ethical behavior and morality, lacks values and standards of excellence in our public schools, and there are too many corrupt elected officials, as well as business leaders. In today's society, bribes and "golden parachutes" seems to be the order of the day. Scandals run rampant and dishonesty seems to be acceptable as the "new normal" way of doing business. Such adult behavior has its roots in the lack of teaching right versus wrong, and need of good role models by parents, *especially* in early childhood years. I know this to be true, because my spouse experienced this lack of ethics in thousands of our youth, especially teens on a daily basis, in her four decades of teaching—and *it is getting worse.*

We rejected Nazism, Fascism, Communism, Racism, Anti-Semitism, and Fanaticism… because they offended our consciences, contradicted our deep intuitions about human rights, and violated our fundamental human values. If we do not reverse the current trend, we will face the next decade, with even greater decay of our American society.

## What Others Think

All behavior of humans in today's Western Society (particularly in America) is based on, or motivated by, the approval and perception of others! That is, "What will the Jones' think?" This is "fear" based on what "others" think or approve—including society in general, disregarding what you may actually "think," "desire" or "feel"! Too many individuals fall into this trap created by society itself, and they condone or accept this role without question. These persons sacrifice their own identity and individuality to the whims of others (like a kind of "quicksand"). They sacrifice their "self-concept" in return for the approval of others in Western society.

The forgoing being the reality of today is a very sad situation. Where are the mavericks, the risk takers, the futuristic innovative "thinkers and doers?" Where are the "wild ducks," that refuse to fly in formation? Where will our future leaders come from? Not from the passive, submissive persons who are the sacrificial lambs, who so willingly submit to others. These persons actually turn over the reins of control to others, the reins of their very lives. They are at the mercy of those who are willing to lead and exploit them for their own desires. *It is manipulation on a grand scale!*

## Goals

One should set one's own goals (mentally and spiritually) in life to achieve happiness. *"Be true to yourself!"* Therein is the key to self-fulfillment and happiness. Anything overriding this goal dooms one to a life of unhappiness! As one is born of free will, who is it that has "freedom of choice," why would one so willingly give up this most precious God-given right by surrendering to the pressures of any group within our society? Even our American Constitution defends and guarantees this most valued right. Astonishingly few exercise, value or assert this right! We truly are becoming *"a nation of sheep!"* Consider other nations in history (USSR, North Korea, Iran, Cuba, etc.) that gave up this right. Where are they today? Will you continue to follow the "whims of society" and turn over your destiny and happiness to the "Jones'?"

The decline of American Culture and Society, when it happens over the next decades, will be due primarily to one or more of the key factors summarized below.

## Beliefs

Psychologist Martin Seligman, in *Learned Optimism* (Knopf, 1991), suggests that the loss of religious belief in the 1960s was partly responsible for the dark mood and (some) national disasters—from race riots, to the Vietnam War, to national disillusionment—of that era. We know, or should know, that grave sin breeds misery, whereas faith and hope breeds optimism. In times of crisis and war, people need God. *"There are no atheists in foxholes,"* someone once wrote.

In times of plenty, they forget God, and worship pagan gods, themselves or "things." Extreme fundamentalism and false religious beliefs are pathological, and have also caused evil in the world. Some examples are past bloodbaths of the Reformation (Thirty-Years War), the Crusades (killing of thousands of Muslims and Jews), Inquisitions (burning of heretics), and recent fanatical religious conflicts between Moslems and "infidels." These conflicts, as bad as they were, cannot compare with the tens-of-millions slaughtered by communism, especially during the "cold war."

Tomorrow's generation will certainly encounter far greater evil forces because of: enormous power of Weapons of Mass Destruction (WMD) in the hands of terrorists; the corruption of the Mass Media by unethical individuals; worldwide water shortages,; New Age movements, and other misguided occults. One or more of these developments will eventually cause a new global crisis, or World War III. Interestingly, Christianity was supreme during earlier times of great adversity, and rarely at its best during times of economic prosperity. These expected times of great crisis, hopefully will once again, awaken the need for all people to seek the Divine Mercy and Love of Jesus Christ.

## Mass Media Mania

> *A climate of opinion, like a physical climate, is so pervasive a thing that those who live within it and know no other take it for granted. The point of great importance is not the experiences on which we have to draw, but our interpretation of it.*
> —Ralph W. Emerson

Whom do you really trust and believe for accurate news about your world? It seems that we have two extremes: Far left "Progressive Liberals," like ABC, CNN, CBS, CNBC, and The New York Times. In contrast, extreme "conservatives," such as Fox News (which claims, "*We report, you decide*"). The Wall Street Journal provides a higher quality, more balanced viewpoint, but its readership is limited to business people. Who is in the middle of these two extremes? It might be C-SPAN and PBS if you want in-depth coverage of an issue. These conflicting news services attack each other, and too often give us distorted views of the real world. One might cry, *just give me the news!*

How many educated listeners can determine, what is truth? Most of the media targets a ninth grade reading level (or lower). Listeners are confused as to who is telling the actual truth. These clashing news reporters purport to be "*the authority*" on what the news really means to its less educated audiences. Some even "manufacture" the news. This is a disservice to the viewing public eager to have just the "truth of the matter" presented to them. It too often becomes a clash of personalities or opinions.

Of course, negative sensational news is what sells in our secular, progressive and materialistic world. Passive reporting of positive events does not sell. This is a psychological fact! It is the "nature of the beast!" How can we change this "mass media mania?" The answer is only by the public *demanding* reasonable standards of excellence!

Meaning is context dependent. Language creates and distorts, discloses and hides, enables and inhibits, oppresses and enriches. Everything that we see and feel with our five senses and scientific instruments is a product of mind and spirit. *Perceptions are conceptions*, mental thoughts not merely empirical truths. We create visions of our empirical world, and if those images match our conception of that world, we "think" we have found truth. There is a hierarchy of knowledge: (1) Matter, energy, and time are the physiological lowest level. (2) Life is the biological level. (3) Mind is the rational and psychological level. (4) Soul is the metaphysical or spiritual level. 5. God is the mystical, contemplative, and theological highest level. All lower levels are transcendent by higher levels that control, synthesize and embrace all lower levels.

## Symbols

Symbols represent a vital means of human communication that has existed for thousands of years, and can significantly help humans to focus their thoughts and prayers. Most of the great works of art and architecture developed from ancient Greek and Roman religious paintings and sculptures. The Church was one of the first patrons of the classical arts, music, architecture, universities, and most of the fundamental sciences, which later became the foundation for all other forms of the arts and sciences.

There are many symbols used in the secular world to represent things, objects and ideas for teaching, for business, and for entertainment. Could television and advertisement industry exist without symbols? Symbols are in many ways part of that which it symbolizes, and calls up the feeling associated with it. Symbols include the cross in a Christian Church, the Star of David in Synagogues, and the Crescent on top of a Mosque. Symbols are a kind of entryway into the culture of a religion— the chain of associations that are endless. Symbols participate in that which they symbolize.

## Communities

In the past, families and small ethnic communities were closer knit to insure their own survival and if they took into account their neighbor's welfare, so much the better. Such is no longer the case in the 21st century. We are now a truly "global society." The population "meltdown" in Western Europe, due to acute birth control practices and aging populations, and the filling of the resulting demographic gap by Islamic immigration, has and will continue to seriously impact, western culture, politics, and religion. This affects economic and social systems, causes severe unemployment and crime among minority groups, and further erodes Christian values and traditions.

## Immigration Challenges

In the United States, the challenge is also dealing with about twelve million illegal Latino immigrants, most of which are Mexicans. More than 15% of the total *legal* population is currently Hispanics. That represents over 45 million people and this growth rate is increasing very rapidly. Hispanic communities are family-oriented, mostly conservative, and Christian. About 70% of all third generation, young Hispanics speak English. Why is this so? They want to assimilate and get ahead economically. Muslim immigrations (representing about 2%) will also become a major future problem.

Governments exist *fundamentally* to provide security and protection for its citizens, among essential social requirements, such as health, which is not a "right," and general welfare. How can our government agencies be responsible for the basic needs of its citizens, especially considering the "war on terrorism," drug trafficking, human trafficking and future pandemics, while achieving these essential objectives, humanly?

First, we must identify, who is who? All illegal Mexicans (all illegal persons) should be given about one year's time (a grace period) to register and receive a tamperproof ID card. We can encourage them to register (the "carrots") by promising to allow all who do not have a criminal record to stay and work for 3-5 years. During that time, they will be entitled to education and health services, and they can file to obtain U. S. citizenship.

Second, enforce this new policy (the "sticks") by severely fining any company that hires anyone (after a one year grace period), without this special ID card, for each abuse of this law. In addition, after this grace period, those without this foolproof ID cards will *not* be entitled to jobs, education and health services (except in emergencies).

Third, those that get the new ID's must learn English, must pay taxes, and cannot be involved in any criminal activity. Education and health services paid by states should be subsidized by Federal agencies responsible for oversight and enforcement.

Fourth, those who refuse to register or have criminal records, and/or are not loyal to America must be exported, *permanently*. If illegal persons cannot find work, have no access to basic services, they will naturally migrate back to their original country.

Fifth, concurrent with this policy, our government must build a physical and electronic fence across the entire border, with advanced technology that can detect all breaches, with guards to protect our borders. This American population will require younger educated workers from other countries. Otherwise, the economic system will collapse. In addition, social security will become bankrupt, without new younger workers.

# APPENDIX

## Food Stamp Program

Source: *The Heritage Foundation* (condensed for this book)

What many may not realize is that participation among able-bodied adults *without* dependents (ABAWDs) has been skyrocketing compared to the total number of participants. In just four years, the number of able-bodied adults without dependents on the food stamp rolls skyrocketed by over 2 million. While overall food stamp use grew by 53 percent between Fiscal Year 2007 and Fiscal Year 2010 (from about 26 million to nearly 40 million), it more than doubled among able-bodied adults without dependents during this time–from 1.7 million to 3.9 million–an increase of roughly 127 percent. Food stamp spending today is roughly $80 billion, double what it was in Fiscal Year 2008.

Going forward, food stamp policy should ensure that resources are going to those most in need—particularly at a time when budgets are tight for so many American Able-bodied recipients should be encouraged to work. This way, help is available to *those who truly need it*, while at the same time individuals are encouraged to do what they can to help themselves. ...

While the recession no doubt plays into the increases in food stamp participation, policy loopholes have opened the doors to boost growth as well. In his 2009 stimulus bill, The [Administration] allowed states to waive the modest ABAWD work provision (which says that after 3 months ABAWDs must work or perform some type of work activity for 20 hours per week to remain on food stamps).

With the work waivers in place, ABAWDs can stay on food stamps for an *unlimited amount of time* without working or preparing for work. Without a work requirement, it is difficult to ensure food stamps are not going to those who could otherwise work. A work requirement acts as a gatekeeper: those who really need assistance can still get it, while those who may not really need it will be deterred, thus targeting resources to the truly needy. It also encourages individuals to move towards work, and it can provide job training and other employment help.

Self-sufficiency for able-bodied adults should be the goal of any sound welfare policy. Unfortunately, most of the government's 80-plus welfare programs—including food stamps—aren't focused in this direction. Helping those in need means **helping them rise above government dependence**. Unfortunately, self-sufficiency seems to be kicked to the bottom of the list all too often when it comes to reforming the nation's broken welfare system. It's time for Congress to realize that helping individuals means a hand-up, not merely a handout.

## Violent Video Games

### More Playing Time Equals More Aggression

COLUMBUS, Ohio – A new study provides the first experimental evidence that the negative effects of playing violent video games can accumulate over time.

Researchers found that people who played a violent video game for three consecutive days showed increases in aggressive behavior and hostile expectations each day they played. Meanwhile, those who played nonviolent games showed no meaningful changes in aggression or hostile expectations over that period.

Although other experimental studies have shown that a single session of playing a violent video game increased short-term aggression, this is the first to show longer-term effects, said Brad Bushman, co-author of the study and professor of communication and psychology at Ohio State University.

"It's important to know the long-term causal effects of violent video games, because so many young people regularly play these games," Bushman said.

"Playing video games could be compared to smoking cigarettes. A single cigarette won't cause lung cancer, but smoking over weeks or months or years greatly increases the risk. In the same way, repeated exposure to violent video games may have a cumulative effect on aggression."

Bushman conducted the study with Youssef Hasan and Laurent Bègue of the University Pierre Mendès-France, in Grenoble, France, and Michael Scharkow of the University of Hohenheim in Germany.

Their results are published online in the Journal of Experimental Social Psychology and will appear in a future print edition.

The study involved 70 French university students who were told they would be participating in a three-day study of the effects of brightness of video games on visual perception.

They were then assigned to play a violent or nonviolent video game for 20 minutes on each of three consecutive days.

Those assigned the violent games played Condemned 2, Call of Duty 4 and then The Club on consecutive days (in a random order). Those assigned the nonviolent games played S3K Superbike, Dirt2 and Pure (in a random order).

After playing the game each day, participants took part in an exercise that measured their hostile expectations. They were given the beginning of a story, and then asked to list 20 things that the main character will do or say as the story unfolds. For example, in one story another driver crashes into the back of the main character's car, causing significant damage. The researchers counted how many times the participants listed violent or aggressive actions and words that might occur.

Students in the study then participated in a competitive reaction time task, which is used to measure aggression. Each student was told that he or she would compete against an unseen opponent in a 25-trial computer game in which the object was to be the first to respond to a visual cue on the computer screen.

The loser of each trial would receive a blast of unpleasant noise through headphones, and the winner would decide how loud and long the blast would be. The noise blasts were a mixture of several sounds that most people find unpleasant (such as fingernails on a chalk board, dentist drills, and sirens). In actuality, there was no opponent and the participants were told they won about half the trials.)

The results showed that, after each day, those who played the violent games had an increase in their hostile expectations. In other words, after reading the beginning of the stories, they were more likely to think that the characters would react with aggression or violence. "People who have a steady diet of playing violent games may come to see the world as a hostile and violent place," Bushman said. "These results suggest there could be a cumulative effect."

"Hostile expectations are probably not the only reason that players of violent games are more aggressive, but our study suggests it is certainly one important factor," Bushman said. "After playing a violent video game, we found that people expect others to behave aggressively. That expectation may make them more defensive and more likely to respond with aggression themselves, as we saw in this study and in other studies we have conducted."

Students who played the nonviolent games showed no changes in either their hostile expectations or their aggression, Bushman noted. He said it is impossible to know for sure how much aggression may increase for those who play video games for months or years, as many people do. "We would know more if we could test players for longer periods of time, but that isn't practical or ethical," he said.

"I would expect that the increase in aggression would accumulate for more than three days. It may eventually level off. However, there is no theoretical reason to think that aggression would decrease over time, as long as players are still playing the violent games," he said.

Contact: Brad Bushman, Bushman.20@osu.edu
Written by Jeff Grabmeier, Grabmeier.1@osu.edu

# GENERIC JR REPORT

IN THE CIRCUIT COURT OF THE SIXTH JUDICIAL CIRCUIT
OF THE STATE OF FLORIDA, IN AND
FOR PINELLAS COUNTY
UNIFIED FAMILY COURT, DEPENDENCY
CASE NO: XXXX DPANO

IN THE INTEREST OF:

Children's Name: Johnny (DOB 02/14/12) SPN: nnnnn A Child

### GUARDIAN AD LITEM REPORT TO THE COURT

Guardian ad Litem: Miriam, M.A., and Robert Fertig

Type of Hearing: Judicial Review     Date of Hearing: mm/dd/yy

Case Plan Goal: Reunification/Adoption

Length of time child in/out of home care: Since mm/dd/yy, about 12 months.

Number of placements: Two: Group foster house, and current Foster Care.

## Recommendations:

**Placement**: Foster care placement should continue. Guardians recommend delaying reunification so that father's case plan tasks can be fully documented, and to give mother an opportunity for over-night visitations with her child.

**Services needed for the child**: Child has a history of problems, including eye, ear and lung infections. Father refused to give child his prescribed medications, when required.

**Permanency**: GALs recommend a Safety Plan for Permanency with child's foster family, if allegations about father's substance abuse and DV are true.

**Domestic Violence:** Father's case plan includes Anger management classes and AAA meetings. No documentation exists that these tasks were completed.

Father's unsupervised overnight visits should NOT continue, until case plan tasks are fully completed and new allegations are investigated.

**Child's Wishes:** Child is too young to express his wishes.

## Timeline to permanency:

**Shelter Date(s): mm/dd/yy**

**Adjudication of Dependency Date(s): mm/dd/yy**

**Current Case Plan Acceptance Date: mm/dd/yy**

**Case Plan Expiration Data: mm/dd/yy**

**Placement History:** According to Hot Line: The child was removed due to Domestic Violence and substance abuse. Mom's prior arrested on was for _allegedly_ punching dad while he was holding the child. She denies everything! The father had two DUI's and lost his driver's license. DMV reports he is a "habitual traffic offender." The child was present during Domestic Violence incidents. Guardians learned that father has outstanding warrant(s) in PA, NC, TX and FL, for failure to support his other children.

The home of the father was messy and it smelled like smoke. The smoke on little Johnny's clothes was so bad foster mother had to change his clothes after he was picked up. Father's previous wife, Maria, claims that all the women in his life have experienced violence, and have dropped charges out of fear. He's a heavy drinker and did cocaine. The earlier mother stated, *"He is not fit to take care of any child."*

**Summary:** As the GAL has been saying throughout this entire case (12 months) – the home environment for this child is not acceptable and the father is in "denial" and does not properly care for his child. The thought of little Johnny not having prescribed medication and smoking in his home, when clearly it is documented that he has breathing problems, should cause everyone concern! ECA needs to look into the future safety of this child.

**Mental/Medical Health: CBHA completed**. Child has had a history of problems, including eye, ear and lung infections. Father has refused to give child prescribed medications, when required.

**Daycare:** The child attends Home Schooling at the Foster Care Home.

## Case Plan Progress:

Current Case Plan Acceptance Date: mm/dd/yy. Child was placed with the father, and later removed to a group foster home, and then sent to the current foster home. Both parents have unsupervised visits.

**Mother's Progress with Case Plan Tasks: Ms. Dolly**

**Parenting classes:** Completed in yyyy

**Psychosocial:** Completed mm/dd/yy with DFL.

**Anger Management:** She claims her lawyer has documented proof of completion.

**Counseling:** She completed 12 weeks at Operation PAR.

**Substance Abuse Evaluation:** Completed with PAR by mm/dd/yy

**RUA tests:** Negative in yyyy; there were two positive swabs that were explained as false positives; additional swabs have been negative.

**Income and housing:** Paramour's financial records verified by GAL; home is without hazards (see recent photos taken by GAL).

**Child visitations:** Typically weekly, unsupervised. Missed two visits; both were for reasonable causes: vehicle accident.

**Cooperate with Guardians:** Yes

**Father's Progress with Case Plan Tasks: Mr. Martin**

**Parenting classes:** No documentation

**Court Ordered:** No Contact with child's mother.

**Attend AAA.** He stopped attending after two sessions.

**Domestic Violence and Anger Management:** No documentation is available. ADR has confirmed father refused to complete courses.

**Family Counseling:** N/A (Court Ordered no contact).

**Random urine drops:** Missed many drops. Lack of documentation.

**Income and housing:** No documentation (requested many times).

**Child visitations:** Typically weekly overnights, unsupervised.

**Cooperate with Guardians:** No.

## Sources Contacted/Consulted:

Case manager, Joe (plus prior two CMs); Father Martin.; Mother Dolly; Foster Care providers; ECA files; Sheriffs' records; former wives and paramours: Jane, Kate, Maria (CA), and Mr. Martin's other son, Andy; ADR; Code Enforcement; and DMV records.

## Summary:

**Home Safety:** Father had a history of safety and health hazards. See photographs by GAL during visits (with father's permission). While some corrections were verified, there remain other threats to the Johnny's health and safety. The Home Study did *not* include background checks with all family members.

**Medications**: Foster caregivers have reported that the child has had eye, ear and lung problems that required antibiotics and Nebulizer, yet father refused to give the child meds, and he smokes. The child has also returned from some visits, dirty and coughing.

The Police removed the child, and arrested both parents. Prior wife, Maria claims: "Martin beat me for two years in Florida. I had to flee to another state to avoid further battering." Police records researched by GAL seem to support her claims.

Johnny is doing well at the current foster care family home. He is actively socializing with their children, playing with them when we visit him every month.

**Respectfully Submitted by
Miriam Fertig, M.A. and Robert Fertig**

# TERMINATION OF PARENTAL RIGHTS (GENERIC)

A Permanency Hearing is required within 9-12 months after removal of the children, and after subsequent JR hearings at least every 5-6 months. The state, GAL and CM advocate for a *permanent* family home for the children, by recommending Permanent Guardianship, or Adoption, *after* TPR. The parents or relative caregivers have 30 days to file a reply to a TPR filing by the CM/GAL. The judge then orders mitigation.

A meeting between the ADA, CM, GAL, the parents, and lawyers for all sides, takes place under a court appointed "neutral" expert, who attempts to mitigate the issues to avoid TPR, if possible. If all sides come to an agreement, they all sign the document, before sending it to the judge for "official" approval. (We have had signed agreements by all sides that were *not* approved the judge).

Afterward, all parties prepare for the TPR trial before the judge, typically within 30-60 days. Attorneys representing all sides (ADA, CM, and GAL), the parents, and the expert witnesses, gather evidence and prepare their clients for trial. The authors have been involved in two TPR trials. *Preparation is crucial!*

A few days or weeks before trial, a *huge pile* of discovery documents arrives for our last minute examination. We had to sift through two feet of papers to find 2-3 key documents; facts that were very relevant to the case. At this *critical* stage, we believe it is best to turn off all phones and find a quiet conference room to go over **ALL** the evidence with our lawyer, to plan our strategy, and finalize our TPR report, in order to win the case for the **Best Interest of the Children**. *Rehearsals are essential!* GAL must *avoid all* hearsay and focus on what we observed? Whom did we speak to (quoting where possible)? The key statement: what our independent investigation shows? In addition, expert interviews or summaries of reports are very important.

Although TPR cases are very challenging to prepare for and win for the "best interest of the children," they usually are "black and white" cases; they are not in the fuzzy area of dealings. If it gets to the TPR stage the parent(s) are **not** doing their case plan, they are **not** cooperating, and they have probably **failed** to care for their children. The GAL, the Assistant DA, the CM and the legal team has to prove the case by *"clear and convincing evidence."* The *alleged* culpable parents are **not** required to prove their case. Defense trial lawyers do not have to provide witnesses or put the parents on the witness stand. Court-appointed attorneys during TPR are typically excellent advocates.

**Post TPR Appeal:** Parents have a legal right to appeal the judge's decision within 30 days. They need a *special* appeals lawyer who argues issues about the law. They don't contest the specific facts of the case; only "interpretation of the law." Appeals can take many months by the higher court. Meanwhile the potential adopting parents have to have great patience, and hope that appeal is denied.

**Post-TPR Review**: The judge then hears from CM and GAL about *permanency plans*, followed by the **Adoption Petition.** Children are officially placed for adoption within six months of termination. GAL requests information on the adoption selection from the CM. GAL may elect to monitor the case, until it is final, or move on to other cases. We believe in staying with a case until *actual* adoption happens because technical details could derail the process. Once GAL requests to be removed from any case—*it's final!*

## Sample Criminal History:

(Note: Due to co-dependency, the mother dropped battery charges against father).

**1. Father, Mr. Ken Robertson:**

03/03—Aggravated Battery on Pregnant Mother (child born 6/19/03):

01/04—Attempted Fraud-Urine Testing

03/04—Possession of Oxycontin

03/05—DV Battery—charge dropped by wife; Grand theft, Felony Battery

04/07—Possesion of Cocaine-<u>Guilty/Convicted</u>

08/07—Cocaine-Felony

12/07—DV Battery by "Strangulation." <u>Felony</u> (Dropped by wife).

02/08—DWLSR-Felony Flee/Elude Police <u>Felony-Guilty/Convicted</u>.

04/08—Possesion Cocaine <u>Guilty/Convicted</u>; Revoked Drivers License.

**2. Mother, Mrs. Cathy Robertson:**

08/02—Battery, Failure to appear Felony, Cocaine.

04/07—Larceny, Battery, Felony, moving Traffic Violation-Reckless Driving.

06/07—Obstructing Justice, resisting Officer with violence <u>Guilty/Convicted</u>

08/07— Reckless driving, Possession Cocaine- <u>Guilty/Convicted</u>

11/07—Vehicle Theft Grand 3rd degree, Cocaine Felony - <u>Guilty/Convicted</u>

01/08—Resisting Officer with Violence- <u>Guilty/Convicted</u>

10/08—Selling Cocaine-Resist Office with Violence <u>Guilty/Convicted.</u>

Typical TPR Report:

COMES NOW the Guardian ad Litem, by and through their undersigned attorney, and files herein: **GUARDIAN AD LITEM TERMINATION OF PARENTAL RIGHTS TRIAL REPORT to the Court.**

**IN THE INTEREST OF: Sue (DOB: 09/03/10) A Minor Child**

<u>**GUARDIAN AD LITEM REPORT TO THE COURT**</u>

| | |
|---|---|
| **TYPE OF HEARING:** | **Termination of Parental Rights** |
| **DATE OF HEARING:** | **10/19/11** |
| **DATE OF REPORT:** | **10/13/11** |

I. Procedural History of the Case
   A. Total time since children was removed from parent's custody: About 08/05/10 – 13 months.

   B. **Reason for removal:**

   1. From 05/20/10 to 07/20/11, the mother was incarcerated. The mother was released into the care of Support Village. The mother had previously tested positive for Oxycodone while residing at the Village. She was on Methadone treatment at

the time of the child's birth. The child was placed in Medical-Foster Care for approximately six months due to **very severe withdrawal symptoms.**

After the mother's release from jail, these Guardians visited her. She did not have stable housing, was living in a condo. She was evicted soon thereafter.

2. The father had been court ordered out of the home prior to the shelter. There were *allegations* of substance abuse. The Mother was pregnant and due within a few months. The mother was on methadone treatment. She had surrendered her parental rights with two prior children in 2005.

3. The father refused a drug test and had a long history of substance abuse. The mother had a criminal history of possession of heroin, marijuana, larceny, shoplifting, and assault. Dad had a criminal history of larceny, shoplifting, violations of probation, domestic battery, fraud, and possession of cocaine and oxycodone.

C. **Dates of Shelter:** 09/05/10

D. **Brief Summary of placements:**

On 6/3/09, the Child was born at Beth Hospital. The child was removed from the mother's care on that date. From 6/14/09 to 9/30/10, the child was at Children's Hospital. She was then moved to Foster Care on 10/01/10 and remained there until 4/29/11. She was then transferred to a second Foster Care placement on 4/30/11 and remained there until 8/11/11. She was then moved to her third foster care placement on 8/12/11 and has remained there until the present day.

E. **Dates of Adjudication:**

On or before 09/07/10.

II. **Guardian ad Litem Involvement:**
   A. Date Guardian ad Litem Program Appointed: 9/20/10
   Contacts with the Parents:

   1. Mother: These Guardians visited with the mother on 11/18/10, 11/21/10, 12/17/10, 3/15/11 and 4/15/11. There was also contact with the mother at court when she was present. The Guardians left numerous telephone messages for the mother, but received one returned call.
   2. Father: These Guardians visited with the father on 9/10/10 and 9/25/10. The father did not keep his appointments for supervised visitation. These Guardians also had contact with him at court hearings.

   B. Other Persons Contacted by Guardian ad Litem:
   Present custodians of the children, Medical foster care mother, The non-medical foster care family, Sandra, Bay Apartments manager, The mother and father, Grace, the child's schoolteacher, and Community Alternatives CM.

   Records and Documents reviewed by Guardian ad Litem: Community Alternatives Reports, Police Reports, County Sheriff's Office, Lab Corp. positive Methadone UAs, Children's Medical Service for the child, CMAT various Nurse Reports. Operation PAR records, Father was positive for cocaine 6/26/11, Mother's Intervention treatment 11/26/11, and Background reports on parents 4/13/11

III. **Visitations:**
The mother and father have visited the children sporadically. Both visited with their child on 11/21/10, 12/17/10, 3/4/11. The parents were asked to leave after fighting in front of the child, according to the supervising caregiver.

IV. **Placements**:
Child is residing in Foster Care. She has lived in this home since 8/13/11.

V. **Services Needed for the Children**:
Child is well cared for now and has no known medical needs at this time. She requires speech development therapy, however.

VI. **Compliance With Case Plan:**
   A. Last Child Welfare Case Plan Reunification tasks approved by the Court on:
   10/16/10.

   Initial Child Welfare Case Plan Target Date for expiration: 07/17/11.

   B. **Mother's Compliance with Case Plan Tasks were as follows**: The mother was given a case plan in order to work towards reunification with her child, and she agreed by signing the plan.

   **Mother Parenting classes: Completed, 1/19/10**

   **Mother Substance abuse evaluation**: Evaluation completed with PAR on 10/26/10. She began WEI Program on 2/22/11. **Unsuccessfully discharged on 5/19/10**. Additionally, the mother has **not** gone for several requested urinalysis. **She tested positive for cocaine in March, 2011.**

   **Mother Maintain stable housing and income: The mother has not provided proof of income to these GALs for the period of 11/18/10 through 11/1/11.** The mother told these GALs that she has been working part-time and that she would provide documentation.

D. **Father's Compliance with Case Plan Tasks were as follows**: **Father Parenting classes.** As of 5/6/11, he had only completed 3 out-of-10. Due to non-compliance with attendances and failure to drop, he was **unsuccessfully discharged.**

**Psychosocial evaluation:** Completed on 3/4/11 with June, LMHC.

The recommendation was for 10 individual counseling sessions. No documentation of completion provided to these Guardians.

**Father Substance abuse evaluation:** The father has completed 5-out-of-10 addiction classes. The father had a negative drop on 5/6/11, but was Positive for Cocaine on 4/26/11. He has not gone for several requested urinalysis as of 6/21/11. He also tested positive for Cocaine in March, 2011.

**Father to Maintain stable housing and income**: He has not provided proof of income to these Guardians for the period of 11/18/09 through 11/1/11. There is no documentation of stable employment. He promised to provide documentation to these Guardians before the trial. He has failed to do so.

**Manifest Best Interest:**
1. The parents **have not** demonstrated the ability or disposition to provide the children with food, clothing, medical care or other care recognized and permitted under state law, instead of medical care, and other material needs.

    **As shown by:** The parents only visited their child 3 times during the months that she was in Medical Foster care. They did attend one of her doctor's appointments. They did not visit her once on her first birthday. They have not paid child support for their child.

2. The parents **have not** demonstrated the capacity to care for the children to the extent that the children's safety, well being and physical, mental and emotional health would not be endangered upon the children's return home.

**As shown by:** The father and mother continue to demonstrate a lack of responsibility. They continue to engage in criminal activity, with the most recent charge allegedly for Aggravated Assault by the father against the mother, who is pregnant. According to police records, both parents were allegedly selling and/or using illegal drugs. Despite being given separate case plans since 2010, the mother and father have not shown the ability to complete case plans. In one year, they have sporadically attended required classes. He has not completed a substance abuse evaluation. He has not fully complied with individual counseling as recommended in a 2010 psycho-social evaluation. Furthermore, their child, born in 2010, tested positive for Methadone at birth. The mother has either refused random urinalysis or not tested as requested by the department at various times. The mother has had sporadic and limited visitation with the children despite the opportunity to visit the children on a regular basis. She has completed parenting classes and has not maintained employment, and she has not maintained stable housing. She has not demonstrated an ability to care for the children as evidenced by her ongoing lack of being able to pay child support as court ordered, and evicted from the apartment for lack of payment.

3. The present mental and physical health needs of the children and the future needs of the child, to the extent that they can be ascertained, based on the present condition of the child are best served by the children being in the custody of the the non-relative Caregiver in Foster Care.

**As shown by:** Both children have thrived within the care of their substitute parents and the substitute parents have ensured that medical, emotional, developmental, and medical needs have been met on an ongoing basis.

4. Significant love, affection or other emotional ties **have not** been observed between the children and the parents. The degree of harm to the children arising from termination of parental rights and duties is considered to be **minimal.**

    **As shown by:** The parents did go their child's first birthday celebration. They did not to our knowledge send a gift. They only visited her 2 times while she was in Medical Foster care. These Guardians did not have sufficient opportunity to observe the parents to form a determination regarding bonding, due to the parents' **failure to keep appointments with theses Guardians.**

5. There **is not** a significant likelihood that the children would remain in long-term foster care after the termination of parental rights in this case.

    **As shown by:** The Caregivers have demonstrated a deep bond with the children and have expressed a **strong desire to adopt the children.**

6. The children have the ability to form a significant relationship with a parental substitute. There **is** a high likelihood that the children will enter into a more stable and permanent family relationship, as a result of termination of parental rights and duties.

    **As shown by:** Both children are best served by being adopted by their current custodians, who have expressed the desire to do so. The children relate to these caregivers as their parents.

Moving these children from their present bonded relationships with their caregivers may cause irreparable harm.

7. The children **have** lived for a period of time in a stable, satisfactory environment, and there **is** a high desirability in maintaining continuity.

    **As shown by:** The child has lived with her custodian about 12 months. Much of her life has also been spent in Medical Foster Care. She is now in a normal home environment with caregivers who love her deeply. Given the child's level of attachment to the caregivers, disruption of their present placements could have deep and lasting effects on the ability to develop and grow into a healthy adult.

8. The child **has** formed a loving relationship with the present custodians.

    **As shown by:** The child has lived with grandfather nearly two years. She has been with various custodians since birth and is now two years old. She identifies her custodians as her parents.

9. The reasonable preferences and wishes of the child, who the Guardian ad Litem deems **not to be** of sufficient intelligence, understanding, and experience to express a preference, **should not** be considered.

    **As shown by:** The child is not of an appropriate age to express their wishes or understand the current proceedings.

10. The Guardian ad Litem has taken into consideration **Florida Statutes (2005), Section 39.810,** as well as all relevant factors in making the recommendation that **parental rights of the mother, and father, BE terminated in the Manifest Best Interest of the Children.**

**Respectfully Submitted, Robert & Miriam Fertig, Guardian ad Litem**

**GAL Conclusion**: The parents had *many opportunities* over the past two years, to complete their agreed case plans. They were about to be reunited with their child on March 1st, 2011. Instead, they (again) relapsed on various illegal drugs, such as Cocaine, weeks before this planned reunion. Now they have been convicted of selling illegal drugs, and dad is charged with aggravated assault against his pregnant "paramour." They blame the Justice System, CM, GAL, and the State, except themselves, for their actions and resulting consequences.

The child has experienced significant physical and emotional suffering. The child deserves **security and permanency** with adoptive parents, who care for their welfare. *Are these parental behaviors examples of responsible, loving parents who cared for their child?*

**We won this case for the best interest of the child. It required a team effort.**

# ILLINOIS DCFS CHILDREN'S CASES

Source: Chicago Sun-Times (Many cases were omitted due to space limitations)

The Illinois Department of Children and Family Services had prior contact with the families of 61 children who died from abuse or neglect in the two-year period between July 1, 2011, and June 30, 2013, with five more cases from 2013 under investigation. What follows are the Inspector General's descriptions of each child's death and the cases still under investigation. Only a number identifies children in the report.

**Children who died from abuse within a year of having contact with DCFS:**

Child No. 2
Age: 13 months
Cause: Blunt head trauma due to child abuse

Thirteen-month-old girl was found unresponsive by her 22-year-old father's 25-year-old girlfriend. At autopsy the toddler was found to have massive head trauma. The girlfriend was charged with first-degree murder. She was indicated by DCFS for death by abuse and for substantial risk of physical injury by neglect to her 3-year-old son, who is now in foster care. She subsequently gave birth to a baby in April 2013; that child is also in foster care.

Prior history: Twenty-four days prior to her death the hotline was called by an anonymous reporter alleging that the father had left his daughter with an ex-girlfriend overnight and two days later had still not picked her up or answered his phone.

Child No. 4
Age: 6 ½ months
Cause: Blunt trauma to the head

Six-and-a-half-month-old infant became unresponsive while in the care of his 19-year-old father. The father called 911 and the infant was taken by ambulance to the hospital. The infant was pronounced dead the following day. The father and 18-year-old mother had taken the infant to the emergency department the evening before he became unresponsive. The infant was observed with no neurological deficits; hospital staff recommended blood tests and x-rays, but the parents refused and left with the baby. A nurse called the hotline and a DCFS investigator went to the home the next morning. The father was indicated for death by abuse and multiple other abuse allegations. The mother was indicated for death by neglect and multiple other neglect allegations. A second child born to the couple in March 2013 is in traditional foster care.

Prior history: The teen parents first came to the attention of DCFS in May 2012 when they brought the baby, then 3 months old, to an emergency department with bruises they could not explain and which they believed might be caused by a bleeding disorder. A nurse called the hotline and the Department initiated an investigation of cuts, bruises, welts by abuse.

Child No. 5
Age: 20 months
Cause: Blunt head trauma due to abuse

Twenty-month-old toddler was found unresponsive by his 67-year-old grandmother when she returned home from volunteering. The 30-year-old mother had left the toddler in the care of her 39-year-old boyfriend while she went to school. The boyfriend was charged with first-degree murder and was indicated for death by abuse. The boyfriend had previously been convicted and indicated for head injuries to a 1-year-old child. An investigation of death by neglect was unfounded against the mother.

Prior history: Hospital staff called the hotline after the boy's birth because they learned the mother had two children in foster care in another state. A third child was in the custody of his father. The mother was indicated for substantial risk of physical injury by neglect and an intact family services case was opened.

Child No. 6
Age: 11 months
Cause: Suffocation

Eleven-month-old infant girl was taken to the hospital by her 39-year-old mother who reported she found the infant not breathing. The mother later confessed to holding her hand over the baby's mouth and nose in order to resuscitate her to get attention. The mother was charged with first-degree murder. She was indicated for death by abuse and for substantial risk of physical injury by neglect to her 3-year-old child who [was] in the care of his father. Six weeks earlier the infant was in the emergency department for respiratory distress for which the mother used rescue breathing. The infant was hospitalized for 2-3 days following that incident.

Prior history: The family first came to the attention of DCFS in May 2009 following the birth of the couple's first child. Hospital staff were concerned about the parents' mental health and a request for child welfare services was made. The Department ensured that the parents were linked with services and the case was closed. In June 2010 the hotline was called after the mother was psychiatrically hospitalized for the second time in one month. The mother was indicated for substantial risk of physical injury and an intact family services case was open until February 2011. In January 2012 the mother's mental health provider called the hotline requesting support services for the family. The referral remained open for one month.

Child No. 7
Age: 9 months
Cause: Blunt head trauma by abuse

Nine-month-old reportedly became unresponsive after given a bottle by her 36-year-old father. The father called 911 and began CPR. During transport to the hospital, emergency responders noted bilateral bruising to the infant's thighs. An MRI revealed bilateral retinal hemorrhages, massive swelling of the brain, and brain herniation. Neither the father nor the 29-year-old mother could provide an explanation for the infant's extensive brain injuries. The family elected to remove the infant from life support four days later. The Department indicated both parents for death by abuse and cuts, bruises, welts by abuse to the 9-month-old and substantial risk of physical injury by neglect to the 2-year-old sibling. The sibling was placed in relative foster care.

Prior history: At the age of three months the infant sustained bilateral corner femur fractures and unexplained bruises. The parents and five relatives had provided care for the infant and the infant's 18-month-old sibling during the time when the injuries could have been inflicted. Both parents were indicated for bone fractures by abuse and cuts, bruises, welts by abuse to the infant and substantial risk of physical injury by abuse to the sibling. The children were placed in relative foster care. At the end of July 2012 the court returned both children home under a pre-adjudication supervision order. The Department was providing services to the family and monitoring the children at home.

Child No. 9
Age: 8 months
Cause: Skull fracture due to multiple blunt force injuries, with blunt force injuries of varying ages contributing

Eight-month-old infant became unresponsive while being cared for by his father. The father called 911 and the infant was pronounced dead in a hospital that evening. In the hospital the infant was discovered to have a skull fracture and healing rib fracture. His three surviving siblings who resided with the 26-year-old parents were medically assessed. The infant's twin brother was found to have head injuries and a 1-1/2-year-old brother was found to have a healing rib fracture. The third child, a 2-1/2-year-old sister, did not have any injuries. The father was indicated for death by abuse and for the abuse of the other children. The mother was indicated for death by neglect and for the abuse of the other children. All three children entered foster care and were placed with relatives. The father was charged with murder. While in jail awaiting trial the father hung himself.

Prior history: In December 2008 the parents brought their 1-month-old son into the emergency department complaining he was constipated. Examination revealed that the infant had a complete break of his femur bone. The parents had no explanation for the injury. They were indicated for bone fractures by abuse and for substantial risk of physical injury by neglect. The baby and his two older siblings entered foster care. The parents participated in services and the four subsequently born children were allowed to remain in their custody while they worked for the return home of their other children.

Child No. 10
Age: 3
Cause: Thermal injuries due to assault with an ignition of accelerant

Three-year-old girl died in the hospital two days after her 29-year-old mentally ill father set his family on fire. Her 33-year-old mother and the father also died. Her 9-year-old brother sustained burns over 35% of his body and survived. He is in foster care with a paternal aunt. On the night of the deadly fire, the children's maternal aunt/relative foster mother permitted the mother to take the children overnight to the paternal grandmother's home where the father was living, in violation of a court order that allowed the mother day visits with the children supervised by the aunt. She also violated a court order that allowed the father to see the children only when supervised by the caseworker. The aunt was indicated for death by neglect to the deceased; burns by neglect to the surviving child; and inadequate supervision and substantial risk of physical injury by neglect to both children.

Prior history: In September 2012 the two children were taken into protective custody and placed with the maternal aunt after their father filled a bathtub with gasoline and threatened to kill himself and the children.

Child No. 12
Age: 3 years
Cause: Blunt force trauma due to child abuse

Three-year-old girl was pronounced dead at the hospital after her legal guardian/aunt and her aunt's boyfriend called 911 because she was gasping for air. The aunt had been the girl's legal guardian since the girl was eight months old. The boyfriend was charged with first-degree murder and is in custody awaiting trial. He was indicated for death by abuse. The aunt was indicated for death by neglect.

Prior history: In October 2010 the Department investigated the girl's mother for medical neglect. Instead of her child entering the foster care system, the mother wanted her aunt and her aunt's husband to adopt the girl. In November 2010 the aunt was granted legal guardianship for one year and the Department monitored the child in her custody for six months. In March 2013, eight days before her death, the Department received a hotline call alleging that the girl was being mistreated by her aunt's boyfriend. A child protection investigation was pending at the time of her death.

Child No. 15
Age: 14
Cause: Stab wounds and drug intoxication

Fourteen-year-old autistic boy was found in his bed stabbed to death. His 50-year-old mother and 44-year-old live-in caretaker were unconscious next to him having taken pills and left a letter explaining their actions. Both women survived and charged with first-degree murder. They were indicted for death by abuse and [also] for substantial risk of physical injury by abuse to the teen's 17-year-old sister who is in the care of her father.

Prior history: In January 2013, the Department opened an investigation of medical neglect to the boy by his mother because she was refusing medical treatment for the boy. During the investigation the mother caused the hotline to be called at least six times alleging misconduct by medical personnel at three different hospitals. The child was released from the hospital to the mother's care with a medical action plan and an agreement that the family would participate in home-based services. DCFS offered the mother intact family services but she refused.

Child No. 27
Age: 4
Cause: Seizure and injuries

Four-year-old medically complex ventilator-dependent boy with a history of seizures was found unresponsive on the floor after his 23-year-old mother and 22-year-old father heard him fall out of bed. His parents called 911 and the boy was pronounced dead at the hospital. The boy had multiple bruises, abrasions, and scars on his body and a laceration on his inner lower lip. The police did not pursue an investigation of the child's death. The Department indicated the parents for death by neglect, cuts, bruises, and welts by abuse, and for substantial risk of physical injury by neglect to the surviving 2-year-old sibling. The Department took protective custody of the sibling, but the court denied temporary custody, instead ordering the family to participate in intact family services. The court case and intact family services case were closed in March 2013.

Prior history: A preventive services case was open from January 2011 until April 2011 when the Department investigated and indicated a report of medical neglect against the parents. The [child] was placed in a children's hospital where he remained for one year. Upon his release from the hospital, he was returned home under an order of protection. His parents were involved in his medical care and he was receiving in-home nursing services. His court case was closed two weeks before his death.

**Cases of children who died from abuse within a year of DCFS having contact with a family member or caretaker of the deceased.**

Child No. 3
Age: 3 ½ weeks
Cause: Suffocation

Three-and-a-half-week old baby died in the hospital two days after being suffocated by her mother's boyfriend's 39-year-old mother (who was not the paternal grandmother). <u>The 14-year-old mother had run away from home with her baby and went to her 17-year-old boyfriend's house</u>. When the maternal grandmother and police showed up at the house to look for the baby, the boyfriend's mother hid with the mother and baby in a basement crawlspace. When the baby cried, the boyfriend's mother placed her hands over the baby's mouth. After the police left and they exited the crawlspace, the baby was unresponsive. The mother was found delinquent of endangering the life and health of a child and was sentenced to 5 years probation. The boyfriend's mother was convicted of endangering the life and health of a child and was sentenced to four years in a correctional facility.

Prior history: In January 2012 the Department indicated a report of abuse to the 14-year-old by her 17-year-old brother, who was a ward. The abuse occurred while the siblings were staying with a sister.


Child No. 14
Age: 5 months
Cause: Suffocation

Five-month-old infant was taken off life support and pronounced dead four days after being brought to the emergency department with multiple head injuries including a skull fracture and severe brain swelling. The 21-year-old mother and 29-year-old father confessed that the father put his hand over the baby's mouth and nose until the child went limp and then they left the baby in the crib until they checked on her later and found her unresponsive. Both parents are charged with murder. They were indicted for death by abuse and for substantial risk of physical injury by neglect to their two surviving children, who are now in the care of the Department.

Prior history: Three months prior to the infant's death, school personnel called the hotline to report concerns about her 6-year-old sibling, who was new to the school. Staff reported that the boy had marks and bruises on his face, neck and arms and after getting sick, he expressed fear of going home early. During the investigation of cuts, bruises, welts, the child denied being mistreated and said the marks were from his 2-year-old brother. The parents denied any abuse to the boy and both the children's maternal grandmother and doctor reported good care of the children, and the investigation was unfounded.

**Children who died from neglect within a year of having contact with DCFS.**

Child No. 19
Age: 2 months
Cause: Undetermined, but apparently sleep-related

Two-month-old infant was found unresponsive in the morning by her 56-year-old maternal grandmother. The infant had been sleeping on an adult bed with her 3 and 9-year-old siblings. This was the usual sleeping arrangement. The grandmother reported the baby never wanted to sleep in her crib. The grandmother and the baby's 24-year-old mother were indicated for death by neglect and for substantial risk of physical injury by neglect to the 2, 3, and 9-year-old siblings.

Prior history: In late May 2012 the grandmother called the hotline to report that her daughter and four grandchildren lived with her and the mother often went out for days at a time without asking the grandmother to watch the children. The grandmother requested child welfare services, specifically counseling and housing for the mother and beds for the children. The child welfare services referral was pending at the time of the infant's death.

Child No. 21
Age: 5 ½ months
Cause: Undetermined, but apparently sleep-related

Five-and-a-half-month-old infant girl was found unresponsive around 4 a.m. by her 13-year-old cousin. The infant had been sleeping with her twin sister in a pack 'n play at their aunt's home. The cousin heard one of the twins crying and got up to check on her and found the other twin unresponsive. The twins were spending the night at the aunt's home; the mother's six other children were at the maternal grandmother's home and the mother was staying with the twins' father. The aunt's husband, who had previously been incarcerated for domestic violence against the aunt and her oldest child and indicated for the sexual abuse of another of her children, was residing in the home. The mother was indicated for inadequate supervision of the twins and for substantial risk of physical injury by neglect to two of her children. The aunt was indicated for death by neglect and for substantial risk of physical injury by neglect to her five children and the surviving twin. The mother's seven surviving children and the aunt's five children were placed in foster care where they remain.

Prior history: In June 2012 the 35-year-old mother and the 34-year-old aunt were indicated for inadequate supervision of the deceased's twin sister. The mother went to get her hair done and took the deceased, leaving the other twin with the aunt. The aunt left the baby in the care of the 13-year-old cousin who took the baby to the beach with the baby's 7 and 11-year-old siblings who took turns watching the baby while they swam. Both the mother and the aunt were indicated for inadequate supervision of the baby five days before the baby's death. The mother was engaged in community services.

Child No. 24
Age: 8 months
Cause: Drowning

Eight-month-old baby was found unresponsive and floating in the bathtub by his 24-year-old mother when she returned home from school. The baby's 30-year-old father had left him and his 2-year-old sibling unattended in approximately 6 inches of water. The father was indicated for death by neglect to the baby and both parents were indicated for substantial risk of physical injury by neglect to the sibling. The father was convicted of endangering the life or health of a child and sentenced to 2-1/2 years in prison.

Prior history: Five months prior to the baby's death, in April 2012, court personnel called the hotline to report an incident of domestic violence to the mother by the father while she was holding their almost three-month-old son. The mother obtained an order of protection against the father, but failed to renew it while the investigation was still pending. The father was indicated for substantial risk of physical injury by neglect and an intact family services case was opened. The parents were referred for domestic violence services, but had not followed through with the referrals before the baby died.

Child No. 31
Age: 3 months
Cause: Sudden unexplained death in infancy, but apparently sleep-related

Three-month-old infant was found unresponsive around 6 a.m. by her 33-year-old father. The father had gone to sleep with the baby on an adult mattress on the living room floor around 2:30 a.m. The baby was placed to sleep on her back on the side of the mattress pushed up against the wall. The father reported she rolled to her side and touched his face. The father, who was living with his sister and was a regular caregiver of the baby, was indicated for death by neglect to the baby.

The father reported that he was not aware of the dangers of co-sleeping. He denied being under the influence of drugs at the time of the baby's death, but he tested positive for cocaine, marijuana, and prescribed benzodiazepines.

Prior history: The baby's half-sister entered foster care in August 2011 when she was 5 months old because the mother had failed to take the child to several scheduled appointments to assess her for sickle cell disease. The mother engaged in services and the child was returned to her mother's custody in March and to her guardianship in November, five days prior to the baby's death. The family's caseworker discussed safe sleep practices with the mother and provided her with a pack 'n play. A caseworker saw the baby with the mother in August and October.

Child No. 39
Age: 4 months
Cause: Undetermined

Four-month-old baby was found unresponsive around 8 a.m. by her 31-year-old mother. The baby was found face up in the mother's queen-sized bed where she regularly slept. There was no crib in the home. At autopsy the infant was found to have congenital heart disease which likely contributed to her death, but because overlay could not be excluded, the cause and manner of death were undetermined. At death the baby had severe untreated eczema. The mother was indicated for death by neglect and medical neglect and for substantial risk of physical injury by neglect and environmental neglect to the three surviving siblings. The father was indicated for substantial risk of physical injury by neglect to the surviving siblings who are in foster care with a maternal aunt. The OIG is conducting a full investigation of this child's death.

Prior history: There was a child protection investigation pending for three weeks at the time of the infant's death. In January 2013, the father of the youngest child and the unborn infant called the hotline to report the mother left the children, ages 10, 2 and almost 2, at home alone while she visited him; that her home was filthy; and that the children complained of being hungry. Despite phone attempts and in-person visits to the home, the child protection investigator had gotten no response from the mother and had not seen the children or been in the home when the baby died. After the baby's death the investigation was indicated for environmental neglect.

Child No. 40
Age: 7 months
Cause: Undetermined

Seven-month-old infant was found unresponsive around 9:30 a.m. by his father. The infant had been sleeping on his stomach between his 26-year-old mother and 34-year-old father on a full-sized bed. He was last seen alive around 7:30 a.m. when he was given a bottle. There was a bassinet in the home. The infant had been diagnosed with RSV (respiratory syncytial virus) two months prior. The parents were indicated for death by neglect and for substantial risk of physical injury by neglect to the mother's surviving children, ages 10 and 11. The two surviving siblings were placed with one of the children's fathers under a safety plan while DCFS awaited the autopsy report. The family decided it was best for him to continue to care for both children. DCFS provided the father with intact family services while he sought full custody of his child and guardianship of the other. The case was closed in December 2013.

Prior history: In June 2012 an intact family services case was opened after the mother was indicated for substantial risk of physical injury by neglect to her two children because of an incident of domestic violence between her and the deceased's father. The couple was participating in services at the time of the infant's death. The intact family services worker had discussed safe sleep with the mother.

Child No. 43
Age: 5 months
Cause: Undetermined, but apparently sleep-related

Six-month-old infant who was born prematurely was found unresponsive in bed with his 35-year-old mother and 5-year old sibling. The mother had breastfed the infant around 9:00 p.m. and laid him between herself and the sibling. She woke up around 3:00 a.m. and found the baby not breathing. She placed the baby in his crib and called 911. The mother was indicated for death by neglect. She reported that she had been advised by the baby's primary care physician and child protection investigators that she should not co-sleep with the baby. During the investigation the father of the sibling sought and was awarded custody of the child in domestic relations court.

Prior history: The mother has a history with the Department dating to 2008 when an investigation was unfounded for environmental neglect. A 2009 investigation was unfounded for a bruise on her four-year-old son's face. A witness said the child fell while jumping on the couch. This child later went to live with his father. In 2011 the mother reported that her then four-year-old daughter had been molested. The report was unfounded after the child denied being molested during a forensic interview. Shortly after the birth of the deceased, hospital staff called the hotline reporting that the mother was acting strangely and threatening to take the premature baby out of the hospital against medical advice. The mother voluntarily underwent two mental health assessments and was not considered to be a risk to the infant. The maternal grandfather assisted the mother in the care of the infant and his sibling and the investigation was unfounded. A month prior to the infant's death, a pizza delivery man called emergency services to report the mother was passed out on a couch with the baby. Police released the baby and his 5-year-old sibling to the care of their grandfather. The report was pending at the time of the infant's death. The mother was subsequently indicated for inadequate supervision. She has no children in her care; both surviving children are in the custody of their fathers.

Child No. 44
Age: 1 ½ months
Cause: Undetermined, but apparently sleep-related

One-and-a-half-month-old infant died in the hospital several hours after being discovered unresponsive by his 34-year-old mother. The mother fed the baby at 4:00 am and laid him face up on top of a pillow with a pacifier in his mouth, next to her on a queen-sized mattress. When the mother awoke at 9:00 am the baby was lying between her and the pillow and was unresponsive. The mother was indicated for death by neglect to the infant and for environmental neglect to her surviving eight children. A short-term intact family services case was opened to help the mother secure appropriate housing.

Prior history: There was one unfounded child protection investigation involving the family. When the deceased was born in April 2013, he and the mother tested positive for opiates and the Department opened an investigation for substance misuse. The investigation was unfounded after the investigator verified that the mother had a valid prescription for opiate-based pain medication for a broken finger she suffered while pregnant. During the investigation, the investigator provided the mother with a portable crib for the baby.


Child No. 45
Age: 6 ½ months
Cause: Asphyxia due to prone sleeping position on a couch

Six-and-a-half-month-old infant died in the hospital 10 days after being found unresponsive during a nap by her 27-year-old foster mother. The 27-year-old foster father had come home from work for lunch. The infant was tired and fussy, so he placed her on her stomach on the sofa to take a nap. The sofa was an L shape and she was placed in the corner with her face facing the back of the sofa. The foster father pushed the ottoman up against the sofa with some cushions to prevent the infant from rolling off the sofa while she slept. The foster father then made a sandwich and went back to work. The foster mother checked on her about a half hour later and found her in the same position unresponsive. The foster mother started CPR and called 911. The baby suffered brain injury related to a lack of oxygen. She was placed on life support which was removed 10 days after the incident. The baby died a little over an hour later. Her mother and grandmother were with her. The foster parents were indicated for death by neglect and for substantial risk of physical injury by neglect to their 2-1/2-month-old infant. The couple's foster home license is pending revocation because of the indicated findings against them.

Prior history: The baby girl's biological parents had three children removed from their custody in January 2010; those children were adopted by foster parents in July 2012. A fourth child, born in December 2010, was placed with the foster parents with whom the deceased was later placed. The biological parents surrendered their rights to the baby boy so the foster parents could adopt him. The adoption was finalized a couple of weeks prior to the baby girl's death. The biological parents were engaged in services and were making progress toward regaining custody and guardianship of their daughter.

**Authors only include "prior history" on the following cases due to space limitations.**

Child No. 46
Age: 1 ½ years
Cause: Hit by minivan

Prior history: The family first came to the Department's attention when the mother gave birth to her first substance-exposed infant, her fifth child, in March 2006. An intact family services case was open until January 2007 when the mother stopped participating in services. The children were cared for by their father and paternal grandmother. In

December 2010 the deceased was born substance-exposed and a second intact family services case was opened. Both parents participated in services. In the month prior to the toddler's death, the mother was noted to have completed treatment and been sober for over a year; drug testing that included screening for alcohol had been negative.

**To be Continued (see many additional cases)...**

# ABOUT THE AUTHORS

**Robert Thomas Fertig** author of, *the Beauty and Wonder of Transcendent Truths*, *a Guide to Universal Truths*, *the Software Revolution*, principal writer of *Waves of Change* and the co-author of *Engineering Workstations*. Robert was President of Enterprise Information Systems, Inc., a Technology Consulting Firm. Currently, he and his wife, Miriam were volunteers for Guardian ad Litem (also known as C.A.S.A.), the objective "eyes and ears" of the courts for America's thousands of abused and neglected children.

Miriam A. Fertig, co-author of *Guardians Without Wings*, retired after 40-years of teaching at Greenwich High School in Greenwich, CT, and the Middle School at St. Paul's, in Clearwater, Fl, where she was voted by her students and peers *"Special Teacher"* in the 2005 Year Book. Miriam received *The 2007 Endowment Chair for Teacher Excellence* for service and professionalism. Miriam earned her BA from Hunter College, in NYC, and MA from Fairfield University, Fairfield, CT.

Fertig's latest books are available from Amazon.com

***Just one new Guardian can change a child's life forever!*** Contact www.guardianadlitem6.org, or call 1-866-341-1425 to volunteer, or to make a tax-deductible contribution.

www.ingramcontent.com/pod-product-compliance
Lightning Source LLC
LaVergne TN
LVHW042244070526
838201LV00088B/15